CHINA TODAY

Publishers of the International Library

LIBRAIRIE ERNEST FLAMMARION—France
VERLAG J. F. SCHREIBER—Germany
(in association with Österreichischer
Bundesverlag, Vienna)
COLLINS PUBLISHERS—Great Britain
RIZZOLI EDITORE—Italy
FRANKLIN WATTS, INC.—
United States of America

International Consultants

JEAN-FRANCOIS POUPINEL—France
Ancien Elève Ecole Polytechnique

KLAUS DODERER—Germany
Professor, Frankfurt

MARGARET MEEK—Great Britain
Lecturer, Division of Language Teaching, Institute
of Education, University of London

FAUSTO MARIA BONGIOANNI—Italy
Professor of Education
at the University of Genoa

MARY V. GAVER—United States of America
Professor Emeritus, Graduate School of Library Science,
Rutgers University

International Editorial Board

HENRI NOGUÈRES
GERHARD SCHREIBER
JAN COLLINS
MARIO SPAGNOL
HOWARD GRAHAM

INTERNATIONAL LIBRARY

NIGEL CAMERON

CHINA TODAY

COLLINS · PUBLISHERS FRANKLIN WATTS, INC.
London · Glasgow *New York*

© 1974 International Library
© 1974 William Collins Sons and Company Limited

First Edition 1974

ISBN 0 00 100140 X (*Collins*)
SBN 531 02712–0 (*Watts*)

No part of this work may be reproduced without the permission of the publisher. All Rights Reserved.
Printed and bound in Great Britain by Jarrold & Sons Ltd, Norwich
Library of Congress Catalog Card Number: 73–21234

CONTENTS

Introduction
FROM THE PAST TO THE
PRESENT . . . . *page* 7

Chapter 1
THE PEASANTS AND THE LAND . 21

Chapter 2
POLITICS AND GOVERNMENT . . 41

Chapter 3
THE CITIES AND
INDUSTRIALIZATION 61

Chapter 4
THE ARTS AND COMMUNICATION 87

Chapter 5
SCIENCE AND ITS APPLICATION . 101

Chapter 6
THE FUTURE 119

INDEX 127

INTRODUCTION

FROM THE PAST TO THE PRESENT

When you read about China as it was before the Communist government came to power in 1949, one of the most striking things to emerge is that the people seemed to be living far back in the past, in contrast to most peoples in Western countries. Yet China was one of the most civilized countries in the world.

The Chinese still measured their year by the moon. As a result it had thirteen months, and sometimes another shorter month was even squeezed in to make up the difference between this calendar and the solar calendar which most other people have been using for a very long time. One of the other obvious facts about China in those days was, as any book by a traveller or historian would point out, that Chinese civilization was very old and was continuous in a way no other civilization still existing could claim to be.

When I went to China, not very long after the Revolution that ended in the capture of Peking by the Red Army and Mao Tse-tung, I soon saw that much of what I had read about it was quite true. While the streets of nearly all the capitals of the world were full of cars and buses and trucks, in Peking there was comparative silence broken by the squeal of wheels that needed to be oiled—the wheels of carts of many types pulled either by animals or by men. People still went about in rickshaws, although the old-fashioned kind in which a man ran between the shafts had mostly been replaced by the trishaw, or pedicab, where the same man pedalled a three-wheeled machine with two seats for the passengers behind him. Most heavy transport was drawn by horse or mule, and there was even an occasional camel train to be seen, bearing loads of goods. It was still common to hear the chant of gangs of men as they hauled heavy carts along the streets of the capital of the world's most populous country. This was a sight, like many others, to be found in Chinese drawings, paintings and sculptures dating back as far as 2,500 years.

At that time, the early 1950s, young girls still married the young men their parents had chosen for them. Generally they had little say and often they had never seen the bridegroom before the marriage day. Most people rarely ate meat, partly because they could not afford it and

A Shang dynasty ritual wine vessel called ku. *During the Shang skilled bronze-casting suddenly appeared and vessels of great elegance and beauty were made*

A Ch'ing dynasty carriage of much the same shape as the covered litter or palanquin

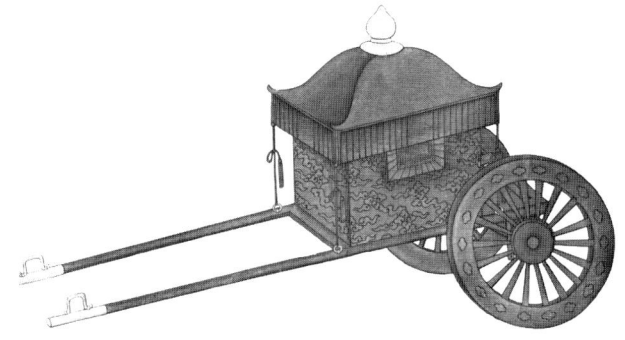

7

In many ways the Chinese population of Hong Kong—four million of them—reflects south Chinese society of the 19th century, and often village society at that. Family-run shops, a closely-knit family system, are still the norm. The rickshaw is disappearing but Chinese festivals are not. Hong means "fragrant" and Kong means "harbour", but the original characters for the place are disputed

partly because it had always been considered a luxury to be reserved for special occasions. No child ever drank milk, because there was no such thing as a dairy industry. A herd of cows was as rare in China as a camel train in England.

The fact that, until little more than sixty years ago, the Chinese were ruled by a system of government which in its essentials had not changed for more than two thousand years, makes it important to know a little bit about the past before going on to understand and appreciate what is happening today.

The very idea that a country should have had the same form of government for so long—as if in England there had been parliamentary democracy with a House of Commons since the time of Christ—is to us astounding. Doubtless this unique feature has something to do with other unusual facts. One is that the Chinese wrote in more or less the same way during all that time; another that the basis of their governmental system was the philosophy of a statesman named Confucius who lived a hundred years or so before the great age of classical Greece.

We in the West are mostly unable to read written material of the time of Shakespeare or to understand the language of writers such as Chaucer without a glossary to explain the meaning of many of the words. And we certainly do not speak the same language as did our ancestors at the time the Romans invaded England. The Chinese, however, can read the written material of ages past and understand it well, for they still write basically the same symbols, called characters or ideographs. They do not need a glossary to understand the poetry of the T'ang dynasty of the 7th and 8th centuries.

The past in China is always looking over the shoulder of the present. How deep its influence is today can be judged by the number of campaigns since the Revolution, which have attempted to alter or eradicate its influence, campaigns such as the one against the 'four olds'—old ideas, old culture, old customs, old habits.

Most of the great and fascinating heritage of Chinese achievement in almost all the activities of mankind can be seen as we look at the various parts of life in present-day China. But just the bare bones of the past should be drawn in now.

The early dynasties

The first historical records in China date from the Shang dynasty which lasted from about 1520 to 1030 B.C., although it was not until excavations during this century that these were proved to be substantially accurate. Writing was already developed, and we know something of the kind of state that existed at that time. Those who could read and write were probably very few, and the majority of the people lived a peasant life. While their rulers could commission the casting of huge bronze vessels for ritual purposes—bronzes that have never been surpassed in beauty and technical skill anywhere in the world—the people were tilling the ground with implements tipped with stone. Their houses were either pits in the ground, roofed with straw, or caves hollowed out of the cliffs of yellow earth, called loess, which covers this part of north central China. This yellow earth has played an important part in Chinese history. It seems to have been blown in from central Asia in the Middle Pleistocene, about two million years ago, and in places it is extremely deep.

In the Shang times, millet was a staple crop as it is still, and the cave dwellings of today are probably not much different from those of the remote past. Perhaps only the *k'ang*, a bed made of brick under which the flue of the cooking fire runs to heat it during the cold winters, is bigger and the cave better equipped. Only recently has the principal hazard of life in this area been largely removed. Silting-up of the Yellow River caused floods which forced the Shang to move their capital several times and made life at certain seasons, when the banks of the river had to be raised, harder than usual. The riches possessed by the Shang rulers, in comparison to the small land area they ruled and the comparatively small population —even taking into consideration the widespread use of slaves—give a picture of massive exploitation of the peasants under a strong patriarchal system.

Confucius— romanized form of K'ung Fu-tzu, meaning "the master K'ung"—died in 479 B.C. His moral and social code became later the basis of government and life in China for more than two thousand years

SHEEP AND COWRIE SHELLS AND BOOKS

Despite the apparent absence of the pastoral stage in Chinese development, it is surprising to note how many words with the meaning "good", or similar meanings, are based on the character *yang* (羊) – sheep;

祥　　hsiang　– felicitous
美　　mei　　– beautiful
羞　　hsiu　　– food
義　　i　　　– virtue, righteousness
達　　ta　　　– first shoots of the grain

On the other hand, it is not at all surprising that many words denoting "value" or "worth" are based on the character *pei* (貝) – cowrie shell, the unit of Shang dynasty currency:

寶　　pao　　– precious
賣　　mai　　– to sell
買　　mai　　– to buy
質　　chih　　– to pawn, a hostage, matter, substance

One of the uses of bamboo was for written records. Slips of bamboo were then held together by several cords to form a "book". Hence the character to be found on the "oracle bones" (卌), *ts'eh*.

The Chinese Dynasties The history of China over more than 3,000 years is naturally quite complex. Dynasties frequently overlapped because one would still be ruling in some part of the vast country while the next held sway in another. But the process can be stated simply in a variety of ways, depending on the aspect to be emphasized. Perhaps the most revealing way is to outline the times when China was unified, and thus show those when it was not. Omitting the legendary Hsia Kingdom of pre-history, we start with the Shang:

Shang (later called Yin) Kingdom	c.1520–c.1030 B.C.	**Third Unification** Sui Dynasty	A.D. 581–618
Chou Dynasty (Feudal Age) Early Chou	c.1030–722 B.C.	T'ang Dynasty	618–906
Spring and Autumn Period	722–480 B.C.	**Third Partition** Five Dynasties Period (three non-Chinese)	907–960
Warring States Period	480–221 B.C.	Liao (non-Chinese)	937–1125
First Unification		West Liao (non-Chinese)	1125–1211
Ch'in Dynasty	221–207 B.C.	Hsi Hsia (non-Chinese)	990–1227
Han Dynasty	202 B.C.–A.D. 220	**Fourth Unification** Sung Dynasty	
First Partition		Northern	960–1126
Three Kingdoms	A.D. 221–280	Southern	1127–1279
Second Unification		Chin Dynasty (non-Chinese)	1115–1234
Chin Dynasty	265–420	Yüan (Mongol) Dynasty	1260–1368
Liu Sung Dynasty	420–479	Ming Dynasty	1368–1644
Second Partition		Ch'ing (Manchu) Dynasty	1644–1911
Northern and Southern Dynasties	479–581	Republic	1912

At this early time the characteristic materials of China were already in use—bamboo, silk, cinnabar. The monetary unit was the cowrie shell brought from the coasts.

The Shang people were conquered by the Chou who came from the area that is nowadays the Kansu-Shensi region. Full feudalism developed under Chou rule, the land being divided into fiefs held by the aristocracy, rather as in England under the Normans. The wealth of the court came from slave, peasant and corvée, or feudal, labour. As a closely knit state the Chou lasted about two hundred and fifty years (about the usual length of later Chinese dynasties), but during the many remaining years of what are loosely called Chou times, China consisted of a mass of contending small states of which Chou was only one. At this time the custom began of dividing the population into four groups: *shih*—lesser nobles and scholars, *nung*—peasants, *kung*—artisans, *shang*—merchants. The last were always despised in China as being non-productive.

Odd as it may seem in this age of turmoil, the Chou was a period of great scholars and philosophers who travelled from state to petty state, taking employment at the courts as advisers. Among them was Confucius—from K'ung Fu-tzu, the Master K'ung—born in 551 B.C., a century before classical times in Athens and about the same time as Buddha in India. He was not an innovator and his doctrine of obedience to rulers, teachers, parents and elders merely made a social code of the existing conditions of his times. But this was to become one of the principal foundations of the Chinese state.

Several other 'schools of thought' flourished at this time, among them mystical Taoism, and the Legalists whose doctrine of authoritarian rule was to be the creed of the next dynasty, the Ch'in. Under their great leader Shih Huang-ti, the country was conquered and unified for the first time as an empire, and the ruler took the title *huang-ti*, or emperor, previously reserved for deities. This was in 221 B.C. A momentous Chinese event had occurred.

The feudal system was abolished, the country was divided into a number of areas, each under the control of a military governor and a civil administrator. Weights and measures, and the length of axles of all vehicles, were standardized, and taxation was levied on crops. Merchants were discriminated against. Tree-lined roads were built, and existing sections of boundary walls were joined up to guard against invasions. The result of this mammoth wall-building was the Great Wall, a defensive barrier but also one that defined the cultural area of China and divided it sharply from the outer, barbarian world. Its building at once passed into Chinese folklore—a symbol of oppression but also of the achievements of the ordinary man.

Shih Huang-ti was one of many rulers in world history who have tried to destroy written material that did not suit their ideas. He burned all the books in the archives except works on medicine, divination and agriculture. But many survived, hidden by scholars. On the credit side, he standardized the written language. On his death, an army officer took over, founding the Han dynasty in 202 B.C. The new capital was at Ch'ang-an (modern Sian) where for the next 1,400 years, with a few breaks, it was to remain.

A 19th-century picture of a coolie (left) and a mandarin in his robes, wearing his beads and carrying a fan. The square of embroidered silk indicates his rank, but only a Western artist would represent a mandarin hatless

Opposite above: the fancy of the Eastern Han sculptor in the 2nd century A.D. placed this fine bronze horse in a flying gallop with one hoof on a bird. It was excavated in 1969 at Wu-wei in Kansu province

The Great Wall of China. Over 2,000 miles long, it was originally built in unconnected parts during the Chou dynasty, and joined at the command of Ch'in Shih Huang-ti in the late 3rd century B.C. Constructed as a defence against barbarian tribes, it served also as a line inside which what was China and Chinese lay, and outside which non-Chinese people were found

The Han made thirteen provinces with boundary lines that have hardly changed until today, and drew the bureaucracy from among the Confucian scholars—another step never reversed until the present. The Imperial Examinations were instituted, their successful candidates forming the learned and governing class. Another class, the eunuchs, first came to the fore as officials in the Han, and was often to play a malevolent role in Chinese history.

The making of porcelain and paper have their origins in the Han, as does paper money. The first recorded journey of a Chinese to the Middle East and back, via what was to be known as the Silk Road, took place. The water-powered mill, the shoulder-collar for horses in place of the strangulating old breast-harness, made for increased production, much of which fell into the hands of the scholar-gentry. At this time, the luxury and the intellectual atmosphere of the court probably outstripped those of any other gathering of people in the world. And in a characteristically Chinese balance, or *yin-yang*, the authoritarian Legalist power of the emperor was nicely allied to its former dire enemy, Confucian bureaucracy.

The T'ang and Sung dynasties

The next crucial period came in the brilliant T'ang dynasty, which lasted from A.D. 618 to 906. Since Han times, there had been partition of the country, reunification and another fragmentation of a hundred years between the end of the 5th and the start of the 7th centuries. With the T'ang, a third reunification took place and a glorious epoch began. While it is misleading to think of change—social or cultural—only in terms of dynasties, at least with the T'ang radical alterations resulted.

Below: this painted pottery hu, *or wine vessel, from the Western Han dynasty, was unearthed at Hsinhsian in Honan province*

A T'ang dynasty vase decorated in san-ts'ai *(three-colour) glaze typical of this period*

First the Chinese boundaries were consolidated, and vast areas beyond them—ranging from Korea in the east to the passes of the Pamir Mountains in the west—were brought within the Chinese orbit of suzerainty. As a result, Ch'ang-an, with its luxurious palaces, became the most cosmopolitan capital city in the world at that time. A turmoil of intellectual, artistic and commercial activity was the context of life there. The streets were thronged not only with Chinese but with Persians, Arabs, Syrians, Central Asians, Vietnamese, Koreans and Japanese. All of them brought their arts and technologies in some measure and also took much from China back to their homelands. Grooms, dancers, singers, musicians, barbers, jugglers, acrobats, merchants—many were non-Chinese. So it is not surprising to find Chinese ceramics taking on the shapes of Sassanian silver, the colours of Persian pottery, nor to find that the hundreds of attendant pottery figures, put into the tombs of the rich to serve them in the afterlife, are often recognizably non-Chinese.

Among the many cultural relics unearthed in China since the war were these painted pottery figurines of acrobats and musicians, dating from the Western Han

Many religions entered China in the T'ang. Buddhism, which had arrived during the Han from India, reached its peak of influence. One of the new faiths was a form of Christianity, Nestorianism from the Middle East, and it gained many adherents. But the Chinese system of rule by an emperor whose mandate came from heaven and not from some religious or other source, and the power of the scholar-gentry whose principles derived from the teaching of Confucius, did not for long permit the growing power of religious organizations. In A.D. 845, the dissolution of the Buddhist monasteries was decreed. "Those who are ... propagators of foreign religions ... shall be compelled to return to secular life lest they contaminate ... the customs of China." This cry, later to be raised against other religions and non-Chinese many a time, is an early example of the concept of the purity,

The Nestorian Stone —a stele discovered by workmen in Sian in 1625. Its Chinese and Syriac scripts set forth the history of the religion in China and its doctrine. This form of Christianity had official recognition along with Buddhism and other non-Chinese doctrines in the T'ang dynasty. The stone is dated A.D. 781 during the reign of the Tê-tsung emperor (A.D. 779–805)

This fragment is from a manuscript of the Analects of Confucius with Annotations by Chêng Hsüan. *It dates from the T'ang dynasty and was found at Turfan in Sinkiang province*

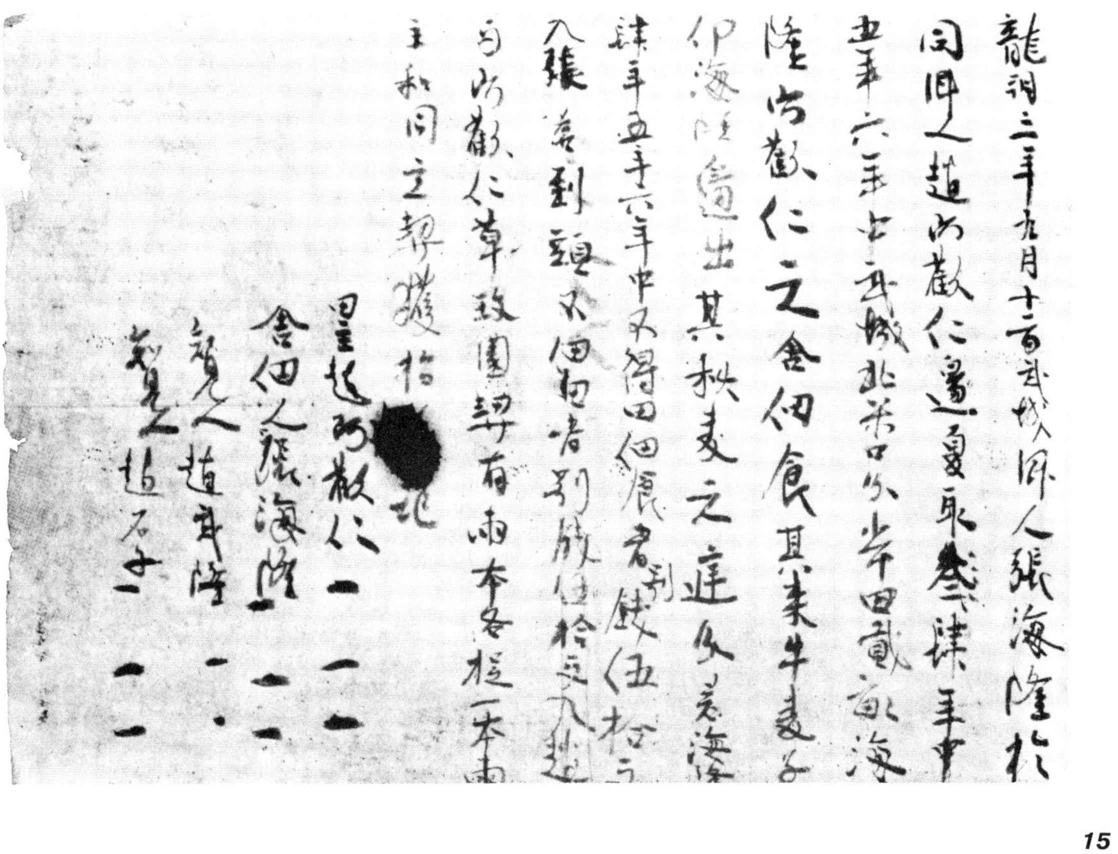

A Sung white-glaze porcelain vase made at the Tsû-chou kilns. It was found at Tangyin in Honan province

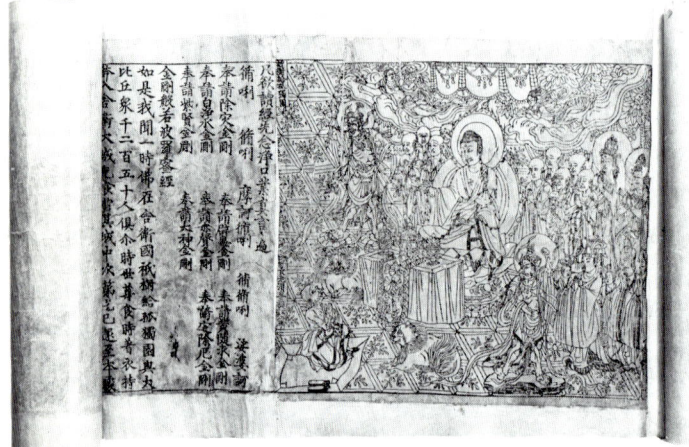

The earliest known example of woodblock printing on paper—the Diamond Sutra scroll, dated A.D. 868 and discovered in northwestern China. It is now in the British Museum

An example of later Ming dynasty blue and white porcelain—a fish bowl of the Lung-ch'ing period (1567–72)

exclusiveness and sacred quality of the Chinese way of life.

Perhaps its poetry is the outstanding T'ang art form. "Whoever was a man was a poet" is of course an exaggeration, but an anthology of T'ang poetry compiled centuries later contains 50,000 poems by 20,000 poets. Yet it was also a time of technical achievement—the length of the year, for example, was calculated as 365·2444 days. The precise tropical year is in fact 365·2421 days. The earliest block-printing known is also a T'ang product—the first example being the Diamond Sutra scroll, now in the British Museum.

The T'ang state broke up into its natural component parts, making way first for what is known as the Five Dynasty period although this is misnamed as there were at least ten entities. Later came the fourth unification of China under the elegant Sung. The outward-looking times of T'ang became the introspective and often self-conscious times of Sung, whose fine arts were perhaps its greatest contribution to Chinese culture. Porcelain and calligraphy-painting reached heights of achievement never surpassed—not even in Japan, China's best pupil in the arts.

It was an age of rethinking and reassessment, of philosophers and great prose-writers, a time when learned men took an interest in the past. Meanwhile the Sung military men were never able to break the strength of barbarian power to the north and north-west. Eventually driven from their capital, K'aifeng, they re-established themselves in the south at Hangchow. And there the court of China attained its greatest sophistication. Not for long, because the invincible Mongol cavalry that had already conquered the world between what is now East Germany and the Pacific soon broke the rule and refinement of the Sung as well. By the latter half of the 13th century, Kublai Khan ruled all China.

Foreign rule

Once more, remote China was opened to the West along trans-Asian routes at first wholly under Mongol control. Travellers such as the seventeen-year-old Marco Polo went to China. Indeed he had been preceded by others wiser than he, but most were merchants, and their little learning was a dangerously inadequate thing when it came to telling the West what China was really like. Marco himself was an employee of the Mongols, and saw life very much through their eyes.

Chinese resentment of the Mongol occupation was intense, and one of the most important results of the century of Mongol rule in China was the consolidation of Chinese dislike of all foreigners. The Mongols were thrown out in 1368 by an uprising of patriotic Chinese led by a former peasant. Mongol Peking was destroyed, and the Peking of the new dynasty (called the Ming, or Brilliant) was built. This is largely the city of Peking existing today, although, as we shall see, great changes have very recently taken place there. It is worth noting that in spite of the humble origins of the new rulers, no idea of democracy occurred to the Chinese. No one thought of anything but to install a new Chinese emperor and ruling élite. There is little sign of developing democracy in Chinese history.

The Ming at once removed foreigners, sealed the frontiers, forbade the introduction of non-Chinese, and also forbade any Chinese to leave the country. It was probably at this time that Chinese ideas, official and unofficial, on the rightness and purity of things Chinese were consolidated. The Chinese had suffered much from tribal incursions over the borders, and much more from the Mongols. All these people were demonstrably less civilized than the Chinese themselves. This led to the formulation of the Chinese opinion that *all* peoples were inferior to themselves, an important point in understanding many of the later contacts between China and the rest of the world.

Oddly enough, during these early Ming times the Chinese admiral Cheng Ho made several epic voyages with a fleet of ships to the South Seas and to India, and explored parts of the east African coast. Unlike the Portuguese, Dutch and English, who were soon to make similar voyages in the opposite direction, he returned not with tales of conquest, but with ostriches, a petty king from Ceylon, and a giraffe. Foreign conquest did not interest the Chinese, partly because, as a later emperor wrote to King George III of England, "we possess all things". China was not only an empire in itself but a nearly self-sufficient nation.

The Ming dynasty was a time of

A Mongol archer on horseback. Genghis Khan, the Mongol conqueror, invaded China in 1213 and his grandson, Kublai Khan, founded the Mongol dynasty

A caricature of a British sailor, published in China during the T'aip'ing Rebellion (1848–65), likening him to a hairy monster. The fumes from the mouth are probably meant to represent tobacco smoke

Lord Elgin signing the Treaty of Tientsin in 1858. The non-ratification by the Chinese of this forcibly extracted treaty led to the invasion and capture of Peking by the British and French, and the destruction of the Summer Palace. Ironically, it was Lord Elgin's father who had saved from destruction the sculptures of the Parthenon in Athens

great achievement, but perhaps its most important aspect was the consolidation of territorial and spiritual China. Long before the last several inept emperors and the decline in power of the administration, however, the Manchu—cousins to the Mongols—had been growing strong. Unified under a single leader they finally breached the Great Wall, and it was not long before they captured Peking and established another alien dynasty in China, the Ch'ing, or Pure.

Chinese males were forced to shave their heads except for the crown, from which a long 'pigtail' grew, thus distinguishing them from the ruling Manchu. Soon the Manchu had made themselves, in all but proud lineage, more Chinese than the Chinese. While the greatest Manchu emperor, K'ang-hsi, who ruled from 1661 to 1722, might occasionally make mistakes in calligraphy, his son and his grandson, Ch'ien-lung, who reigned in the following seventy years, certainly never did.

China and the West

Western Jesuits had penetrated Peking in the late Ming, and under a succession of brilliant mathematician- and astronomer-priests, the Christian cause prospered a little. It foundered eventually in the Ch'ing because the pope of the time attempted to put K'ang-hsi right on the Chinese practice of reverence for their ancestors. Christianity made no headway until the mid-nineteenth century and before then most of its priests in China were imperial employees—technicians and artists. But a Belgian Jesuit Ferdinand Verbiest assisted in negotiations that led to the first treaty the Chinese ever signed with a foreign power—the Treaty of Nerchinsk of 1689 which settled Sino-Russian border problems at that time.

It was at about this time that the West began persistently knocking at the door of China. Portuguese, Dutch and British merchants all tried to trade, finding to their astonishment that China did not want to trade. Magnificent Western embassies were sent round the globe to China, achieving almost nothing in the face of Chinese opinion that foreigners were barbarians.

It was the British who discovered one commodity they could sell to China—opium, an illegal import. Thousands of acres were soon under opium in parts of India ruled by the East India Company, and the product was smuggled into China in ships chartered by that company. By the early 19th century the situation had become electric, and the destruction of quantities of opium by an Imperial Commissioner from Peking was made the excuse by the British for the first of the "Opium Wars", the chief result of which was the imposition of a series of "treaties" on China by the British. These did not forbid the import of opium, opened various Chinese ports to foreign trade, and forced the Chinese government in certain circumstances to favour foreigners rather than Chinese citizens. The Chinese, not unnaturally, still call the treaties "unequal".

In 1860, Peking was invaded and occupied and the Summer Palaces destroyed by an allied British and French force to ensure the ratification of another treaty. China had become a semi-colony of the Western powers. The Chinese government having been brought to its knees, had then to be supported since it could be made to lay further golden commercial eggs in the form of trade privileges.

The serious T'aip'ing Rebellion, which raged in China for fifteen years at about this time, was put down with the assistance of American and British mercenary officers, such as General "Chinese" Gordon. But the Mandate of Heaven of the Ch'ing emperors was running out. Increasing chaos in China was aggravated by the activities of Westerners—of merchants and missionaries. The final straw was the failure of another patriotic rebellion to achieve its object of "driving the foreigners into the sea". This was the 1900 Boxer Rebellion. When the siege of the Western legations in Peking, which the Boxers had mounted with the help of the Manchu government, was relieved by an Allied force and Peking was once again occupied by Western troops, another treaty was signed that finally placed China economically in Western hands. The Allied powers proceeded to its commercial rape, and the dynasty, no longer credible in Chinese eyes, fell in 1911. More than two thousand years of dynastic rule came to an end. China was bewildered.

Republican China

The Republic of Dr Sun Yat-sen that took over, never managed to control the north of China, and soon the country was in the grip of ever-changing groupings of warlords—of whom Chiang Kai-shek was the most successful. In the quarter of a century before World War II, China was laid waste by contending armies, often backed by Western guns, as various powers attempted to be on whichever side won. Into this scene of national misery and untold carnage the Japanese sent their armies, slowly gnawing their way into the suffering hulk of China.

It was in this environment, and stimulated by the obvious necessity for radical change, that the Communist Party, founded in 1920 in Shanghai, gradually increased in strength. The Red Army began to take control of various regions. The first steps towards introducing the peasantry to socialism were taken—redistribution of land, the army working when it could in the fields, attempting to root out the age-old Chinese opinion that the soldier was one of the lowest forms of human life. During the anti-Japanese war, the Red Army did most of the fighting, although it was faced all the time by the attacks of the Nationalist forces under Chiang.

In 1949, Mao Tse-tung proclaimed in Peking the setting-up of the People's Republic of China. An honest administration took over, offering among other things to a starving and hopeless peasantry the chance of human dignity.

The 2,000-year-old way of Chinese life that had ended in tragedy entered the present.

A contemporary impression published in a French magazine of fighting during the Boxer Rebellion in 1900

The tomb of Dr Sun Yat-sen who died in 1925, fourteen years after he established the Republic of China

CHAPTER ONE

THE PEASANTS AND THE LAND

For many people in the West, who know neither China nor any form of socialized organization, the word "commune" has a sinister ring. All the hoary old tales of millions of farming people herded into dormitories segregated by sex, of wives separated from husbands, children forcibly parted from parents and drilled in some grim academy of political fear—all this stock-in-trade of the less responsible newspapers and popular journalism has left its mark on the memory. The fact that no traveller to China since the communes were formed in late 1958 has ever experienced such things and that common sense makes it highly improbable that any system known to man could effect this horrible change among over 600 million peasants by any means whatever, is less dramatic and does not wholly succeed in undoing the mischief.

Mischief it is, for there is nothing at all sinister about the communes. Farm work is hard anywhere in the world, no less so in the temperamental climate of China. The difference between now and the old small-holding peasant economy of the Chinese countryside is almost incredible, yet one of the constants is certainly hard, back-breaking manual work for the peasants. But nowadays, allied to this labour goes the knowledge that the work benefits themselves, their friends, the neighbourhood, the county, the province, and the general level of wellbeing in the country at large. This outlook is encountered everywhere among the peasants today, the result of a transformation in thought that has to be accepted because it is a fact. The communes are run basically by the peasants themselves. They are a logical outcome of the first mutual aid teams that got together just after Liberation in 1949, teams that later on became collectives. The collectives merged, by what in China seems to have been an inevitable and largely spontaneous process, into the communes. The origins of the process lie in pre-Liberation days, in the areas controlled by the Communists where land redistribution and early socialist change had already taken place and made a demonstrably better livelihood for the peasants.

Visitors to a commune, or any other institution in China today, are greeted by the members of the management committee and taken to some room where tea and cigarettes are offered and compliments and polite questions exchanged before getting down to business. Once begun, the order is always the same —first an outline of the past before Liberation, then the process whereby the present came about, and a detailed breakdown of what is happening now; plus the appropriate

A field of rape in flower in Kansu province. Rape is a plant similar to turnip but is grown mainly for its oil-producing seeds

Strengthening an earthen dyke. Manpower is still the most important resource in rural China

quotations from Mao Tse-tung, which are the basis of all action and reaction in thought and argument. Sometimes I was reminded by these quotations of useful maxims from my schooldays—and in fact this is how the Chinese tend to view them, in terms of how to decide and what to do.

We do not have to follow the visitor's routine here, so we can begin where his visit eventually takes him, to the villages and fields, dipping back into the story of the past when it seems appropriate.

Commune life

The little village of Chiaoli lies huddled on a plain with a few low hills around. It is not far from the county town of Teching in Chekiang province, about forty or fifty miles distant from Hangchow, that city of almost legendary beauty extolled not only by the Chinese poets but by such Western merchant-adventurers as Marco Polo.

Chiaoli forms part of the Chengkuan People's Commune, and its inhabitants are one of the production teams in the Bright Star Brigade of that commune. The village is the home of 55 families who have lived there, generation after generation, in the old grey-walled houses with slightly curving black-tiled roofs. It looks somewhat sombre, as do many other Chinese villages—for there was never anything to spare to make them beautiful. A small river, tributary of the Tiaohsi, runs through the village. The land in these parts has always been considered good, and the area is locally called "the land of fish and rice".

In late winter, just at the onset of spring, the small low hills of the district are clothed in the fine reds of the wild azalea, and the peach and plum trees with their thin black angular twigs are sprouting clusters of delicate blossoms. The mulberry trees have begun to deck themselves in clear new green. In the fields, the heads of the barley crop are heavy, moving ponderously in whatever little air stirs. And the fields of flowering rape, whose seeds yield oil and whose leaves make good fodder, stretch like long banana-yellow carpets towards the horizon.

It is beginning to be ploughing time in the paddies, and a few tractors are at work turning green manure into the soil in preparation for the flooding of the fields and the spring rice planting. Soon, when the rape seed and barley are harvested, ploughing will begin in earnest.

The 55 families of Chiaoli number 253 persons in all, and the villagers farm just short of 67 acres (27 hectares) of land. Chinese land is measured in *mu*: 6 *mu* equal 1 acre, 15 *mu* equal 1 hectare. From it they wrest 580,000 *jin* of barley and rice annually—one crop of barley and two of rice. One *jin* equals 1·1 pounds or 0·5 kilograms. There is always plenty of work on the farm, especially now that it is part of a larger whole, the commune. But the heaviest work comes for Chiaoli in May. The barley must be harvested and the early rice planted in the prepared and flooded paddies, shoot by shoot, and then tended with care, weeded, and watched like a newborn child.

Like most rural communities in the West before the effects of the Industrial Revolution fully appeared, Chiaoli is a quiet enough little place with few amusements except those of its own devising. The county in which it is situated runs a mobile film projection unit that goes from village to village and sets up its

Rice-planting in Yunnan province near the Burma border. New technological methods have replaced some manual tasks, but others are still more efficiently carried out by hand

Ploughing at Chiaoli with small Chinese-made tractors

Work on barren desert-land reclamation carried out by students of a school for cadres not far from Peking. These schools were formed to correct bourgeois attitudes developing in people with power and position. Managerial and scientific workers, and others who do not work with their hands and alongside the masses of the people, show tendencies to think themselves better than those who do

screen, projector and loudspeaker in whatever space can hold most of the villagers—generally a street or open space, such as the new sports ground with basketball posts at either end. Provided it does not rain, the villagers do not mind sitting in the open—even in the freezing temperatures of winter evenings—to see the latest newsreels of what is going on in other communes, in factories, and in the great cities where delegations from far countries come and go, and where a whole life goes on that villagers a decade ago had never more than imagined to exist. And occasionally a travelling opera group or a company of jugglers and acrobats comes to the village.

Every house in Chiaoli has been wired to the central radio so that each family can listen in its own home to news bulletins, weather forecasts (so important for a farming community), music and political speeches. The radio also serves as a clock, for even now few people have either clock or watch. In the early days of the communes what was called the "military style" used to be the custom. This term meant that at the sound of a bugle or a bell in the morning all the team members would congregate and set off at a quick march to the fields. In this way they could be sure that, after what might be quite a long walk to reach the place where work was to be done, one vital member was not discovered to be late or missing. But the military style seems less in evidence nowadays, although wherever there is some special project such as the digging of a new pond or dam-building, a little grove of brave red flags flutters hearteningly at the site. Curious, the effect of those flags—the visitor feels it also.

By six in the morning on most days, the villagers have heard on the radio the news and weather reports and are off to work in the fields. Aside from major ploughing and planting, there is plenty of other work to be done. The brilliant emerald-green beds of tender rice seedlings need constant care to ensure that the water in them is at the correct level, that no foreign seedlings grow among the delicate shoots. In the rooms where the silkworms are busily feeding on mulberry leaves and forming the vital cocoons, the earthen floors and the trays on which the process goes on must always be kept clean and fresh. The larvae must be killed before they turn into butterflies and split the cocoons; and the earthen stove that supplies heat to maintain a constant temperature has to be fed. Then there is the eternal chore of collecting what is generally called "nightsoil"—human excreta—which has to be properly processed before use as manure for the crops. At least three pigs are kept by every household in Chiaoli. They are valuable as a source of income, and as a source of manure. Formerly pigs were kept in the village or near it, but now they are generally kept at points nearer to where the manure will be required. Pigs have to be fed and washed down now and then; and the few sheep and chickens that most families also keep need attention too. These tasks are usually performed by a grandparent too old for regular work in the fields, or by some other old person if the family has no older relatives. Very small babies are cared for by their mothers until such time as a relative can look after them or until they are of an age to go to kindergarten. The village has a small primary school on its outskirts and all school-age children attend.

By noon, or a little after, everyone comes back to the village for the

Students at a training college test the quality of rice

Children in a school for the deaf near Canton, learn to form sounds

midday meal, and usually it is two or three hours before they return to the fields. In the hot and exhausting summer days many people take a nap, but there are always things to be done in and about the house. Once the women had to husk rice every day, but now the village has a husking machine that is operated communally. Formerly no household ever had a sewing machine, but now thirteen of the fifty-five families do. And for those who do not, making and mending of clothes can be done for a small fee by the brigade sewing group. Firewood used to be collected by women or children in the hills, now it is communally collected and shared out. Formerly there was no doctor or medical treatment, even for those few who could afford such luxuries, nearer than the county town; now the brigade free clinic is a few minutes' walk away.

By sunset the work of the day is over and everyone returns home for supper. After that there is the radio to listen to, and three nights a week commune members attend discussions on whatever problems have arisen in connection with the running of the farm. Others attend the local night-school classes held in a village house where a blackboard hangs on one wall of the living-room. The classes include political study, technical subjects connected with farming, and literacy classes for those who need them.

Throughout the year there are various holidays besides the regular one day in ten for all. Many of these are traditional, such as Chingming, when the moon is "clear and bright" (what Chingming means). This was formerly the time when families went to clean the ancestral graves and to make sacrifices of food and burn incense. On the commune

A typical group of building workers take a tea break

it is still a holiday, and a specially happy one for it comes in early April just before the spring ploughing must begin. Many people go visiting their friends in neighbouring villages of the commune, but the older people tend to stay at home to make the traditional sweet rice cakes and *tsungtzu*—dumplings of glutinous rice filled with sweet date paste —that are offered to visitors. And of course the day is marked by other extra food and delicacies. The Chinese, until recently, did not have a dairy industry, so they virtually never ate beef or had milk products. Their consumption of meat was always small, the occasional piece of pork, chicken, duck or goose being viewed by all except the wealthy as a luxury. Now they have more, but still not plenty. The main daily food is rice, cooked in many different ways but often just plain boiled, with fresh vegetables of many kinds, pickled vegetables in the seasons when fresh are scarce, various seasonings and sauces such as soya. By Western standards it is a dull diet, filling and unexciting. But it probably resembles that of the Western peasant before industrialization, except that he had beef and dairy products to some extent to supplement his bread, potatoes and cabbage.

Holidays, of course, are times when villagers wear their best clothes. By Western standards again these are few, but nowadays everyone at least has a spare set of clothing for summer and also padded clothes for the hard winter weather —which was certainly not the case before the Revolution. One family in the village recounts how in the old days they were so poor that they could not afford a new mosquito-net, and the old one, patched with cloth and even with paper, served three generations in succession. By the time of the Revolution it weighed

Tibetan peasant women learning to read and write—part of the huge effort to integrate long-antagonized minorities

Grandmothers often look after young children to let mothers go out to work

several pounds! The use of flowered cotton prints for women's clothes is much more prevalent now as more of these come on the cheap market, but until recently the conservative outlook of poor peasants still made even holiday clothes the blue or black or brown of peasant tradition. Few people except the aged now wear the old canvas shoes whose soles were made of any old rags stuck layer upon layer and stitched together. They have been replaced by leather, plastic or rubber shoes, or boots for working.

How communes came about

A village such as Chiaoli is only one of many similar units that make up a commune. To understand how the communes came into being, and why they are such an important productive and economic step forward in the lives of the peasantry of China, we have to take a brief look at the conditions in the countryside at the time of Liberation in 1949. At that time, and for many a decade previously, the peasants' lives were really at the mercy of the landlords and the rich peasant proprietors. The majority had no land, or so pitifully little that it would not have fed a single mouth, far less a whole family. They had to work as hired hands on the landlords' lands, or, if they held land, they did so only by paying 50 per cent or more of their annual crop to the over-all landlord. The landlords were usurers, and anyone who needed a loan—to buy seed, to marry off a daughter, to bury a wife—had to borrow at high interest rates from the landlord. The present village head in Chiaoli inherited a debt to the landlord which had been contracted by his grandfather. Initially the sum was 30 silver *yuan*, but when he inherited it he was owing 170 because the family had been unable to pay the interest in full. Like many others he was born with the debt of two generations on his back, without hope of ever being able to pay it off.

The year following Liberation, land reform was carried through at the instigation of the central government. The peasants burned the title-deeds of land and also the documents dealing with loans from the landlords. In their desperate anger, all over China the peasants put the landlords on public trial, confronted them with their extortionate usury, their plunder of the harvests, their rape of village girls, their beatings of debtors. Many landlords were executed, others allowed to work as ordinary peasants and excluded from the benefits of the new society until they showed signs of accepting its conditions.

After this, mutual aid teams were formed. In Chiaoli, the first consisted of eighteen families who, in 1952, banded together and shared their implements, assisting each other to farm the land they now owned. They elected a young former hired hand to be village head, and collected thirty *jin* of rice to sell in order to buy seed and a few more implements. Their first harvest was the best ever known in the village. Then more families joined in mutual aid teams, and later all the teams joined to form a co-operative—at first semi-socialist, and later fully so.

The advantages of co-operatives over smaller units were obvious. Much larger schemes could be undertaken—the building of small dams, and the effective strengthening of river dikes in times of spate. The pooling of equipment meant more flexibility in its use in a land still badly short of hardware of all kinds.

Here it may be useful to leave Chiaoli for a moment to consider

A member of the imperial family and his wife in their robes. These differ from the robes of mandarins, both military and civil orders of whom were divided into nine grades, each grade reflected in a differently designed plaque on the chest and back, and by different buttons on the cap

what was actually happening in China, for the changes taking place have no precedent in history. The largest agricultural population existing in any one country, and before the Revolution certainly one of the most oppressed, had liberated itself by comparatively simple means. In eight or nine years the peasants all over China had entered the stage of co-operative work whereby thousands formed groupings to share whatever means of production and whatever lands they had. All the old petty boundaries, whether of traditional "back-garden" plots of land or traditional village extent, were eliminated in favour of logical organization and rational farming of the land. Already, huge schemes had been undertaken, such as altering the course of smaller rivers to straighten out their meanders, building canals for the irrigation of lands never before watered, setting up small workshops and factories to mend and even to make new farming implements—and many more.

On a commune where I stayed for some time, they showed me with great pride a strange contraption of wood which could be pulled by hand in the flooded ricefield. It was one of the most ingenious things I have ever seen. Rice—from time immemorial—had had to be planted by hand, shoot by shoot, the planters bent double in the field up to the knees in muddy water. This was a machine to plant the rice shoots automatically. The local carpenter and a couple of other villagers thought it up and made it in their spare time. It was at moments like these that I realized how it came about that until sometime in the 17th century, Chinese scientific achievement was far ahead of that of the West. Chinese peasants, just to take one example of a useful farm machine, invented the wheelbarrow nine or ten centuries before it was known in the West.

In Chiaoli, the rise in actual production since changes in the style of farming, the increase in terms of how many *jin* of grain to the *mu*, demonstrated to even the strongest traditionalist that the new methods were superior to the old. There were hard times. Droughts, floods, occasional blights still affected areas of the land and food was not always plentiful. But the ancient spectre of starvation that for centuries had driven whole villages, and even the population of whole areas, to move away in search of some unknown but hopefully

A simple "crane", really a lever, used by peasants to reinforce the river bank with stone. The river, the White Dragon in Kansu, was notorious for flooding, and the dike-building reclaimed 494 acres (200 hectares) of good land

A dam and hydro-electric power station on the Sungari river in Manchuria. Originally built by the Japanese in 1937, the power station has been extended, using Soviet-type automatic hydraulic turbine generators, and now has a total capacity of 567,000 kilowatts

better place, had at last disappeared. Everyone had food, everyone had a roof under which to live, everyone had clothing.

By early August 1958, there was a general trend within thousands of co-operative farms the length and breadth of China towards combining into larger units. The reasons were many. One was the question of centralizing controls, another how to set up or build large sources of power such as hydro-electric plants, and how to distribute the power rationally among co-operatives when there was no centralized framework. There was also the problem that in some places mineral resources had been traditionally exploited by the peasants at times when farm work was slack. But now that so much reconstruction and new building on and about the farms was in progress, either the agriculture or the mineral working tended to receive undue attention, thus unbalancing the economy of the collective.

During this late summer and autumn, Mao Tse-tung and members of the Central Committee of the Chinese Communist Party spent a lot of time visiting all parts of China to see for themselves what was going on. In August 1958, several co-operative farms in Honan province joined and formed a people's commune, calling themselves the Sputnik Commune. And about that time another series of co-operatives in Shantung province joined and called themselves a state farm. Mao told them that what they were doing was confining themselves to agriculture, whereas they ought to consider absorbing local industry and trade, and should be responsible for local defence as well. That, he said, was something more like what seemed necessary. This remark was widely published and heard by everyone on their radios. Already discussions had been going on at an almost feverish pace among peasants and Communist cadres—the difference between the two being only that cadres are members of the Communist Party, who in the country are mostly peasants—about what were at that time often called simply enlarged co-operatives, and all this activity contributed to what happened next.

Between August 1958 and the end of that year nearly the whole of China's peasants had organized themselves into communes.

As an example of what this meant in practice, a summary of the constitution of the Sputnik Commune, at that time an organization of 43,000 people in four townships, tells quite a lot. Eighty-five thousand people from all over China came to visit Sputnik in its first six months to see what was happening and to assess whether events there would fit their own areas. Sputnik's constitution stated that the commune was a basic unit of society whose task was to manage all industrial and agricultural production, trade, cultural and educational work and political affairs within its sphere. It provided for a "system of citizen soldiery"—the people's militia in embryo. All members over sixteen had the right to elect management, to be elected, and to vote on all commune questions. Property turned over to the commune was taken as "share capital" as it had been in the co-operatives, but anything over a modest amount was "investment to be repaid".

The task of the commune was to promote "an expanding agricultural output . . . to build industry as rapidly as possible", together with roads, waterways and modern communications. The commune took over the local services of the state bank and trading organizations, and it absorbed local government. Members were to be paid according to work, and a wage system would be introduced when "income stability" in the commune had been achieved. This replaced the system of paying for workdays that were reckoned at harvest time. Canteens were to be established to free women for farm work, but "members need not use the canteen . . . service if they do not want to". Universal compulsory education, health services and what are called "happy courts" for the aged were to be provided.

It will be obvious to anyone with some knowledge of and experience in economics and social organization that this constitution was biting off rather more than the commune was likely to be able to chew immediately.

The first Central Committee statement of policy on the communes did not come until there were many in existence. It is a considerably more conservative document than the Sputnik constitution. Issued at the end of August 1958, it remarked that "people's communes . . . have made their appearance", and that it was highly probable that "there will soon be an upsurge". Because, it continues, "of the unprecedented advance . . . in farming . . . and the demands of rural industry for manpower . . . this new form has become the proper form to accelerate socialist construction . . . and carry out the gradual transition to communism."

There was no mention of free food in it, but, as one writer has said, within a month communes all over China were making the happy assertion that to China's peasants even wages were less important than the great dream that nobody should be

Newly trained tractor drivers exchange experiences at the tractor station at Machiao Peoples Commune on the outskirts of Shanghai

A typical peasant house in Taichai Brigade, part of a famous commune in Shansi province. Note the ubiquitous k'ang —the heated brick bed—which fills half the room and the glazed windows which are entirely new since the Revolution

hungry and that the famine of centuries was conquered at last. The months that followed brought curious and often comical effects as communes organized and experimented with the new free-form organization, and discovered that free food, free haircuts, toothbrushes and such like, were not quite within the budgetary possibilities yet. A

improvements of the most fundamental kind, she and everyone else realized that they still had to struggle for their better life.

So, gradually, the communes settled down. The original 26,500 communes were for the most part found to be burdensomely large, containing as they did about 5,000 families in each. By now there are

woman in Chiaoli village summed it up when she said: "We had thought that once we poor people were liberated and became our own masters, our life would naturally become better and better, and there would be no more trouble ahead." While she was enthusiastic about

about 75,000 communes containing altogether 4,800,000 work-teams of between 40 to 60 peasants each, working about 50 acres (20 hectares) of land. The basic accounting unit is the village work-team which is responsible for all that it does, all that it achieves, or fails to achieve.

The practical advantages

Returning to Chiaoli village and the part it plays in the Bright Star Brigade of Chengkuan Commune, it is interesting to see what the production figures are and how the village manages its finances.

Under the old landlord rule, the average yield of grain per *mu* was about 200 *jin*, of which 60 per cent went to the landlords. Peasants who had insufficient grain to live on, had to borrow from the landlords or rich peasants at 100 per cent interest —in other words a peck of grain borrowed one year had to be repaid by two pecks the next.

In 1971, the average grain yield per *mu* was 1,445 *jin*, making a total grain production of 577,060 *jin*. The silk harvest was 12,000 *jin*. Together with other sideline products, the total value of production in the year was nearly 88,000 *yuan*. There are 253 people in the village to be supported by this production. The policy that guides the dividing-up of income takes note of three things: the interest of the state, that of the team, and that of the individuals. In 1971, the grain was distributed thus:

Total production	577,060 *jin*
Agricultural tax (the sole tax, at 3·85 per cent of total income) and the quota of grain sold to the state	253,190 *jin*
Amount reserved for the use of the team	121,670 *jin*
Amount distributed among team members	202,200 *jin*

The year before, during debates among the team members, many were in favour of selling more grain to the state as each member had surplus grain in his home store, while others recommended a large increase in the accumulation fund to buy more farm machinery. Still others thought that a larger cash income per family would be beneficial. Due consideration was given by the management committee to all proposals, and finally with the help of the accountant they came up with detailed plans for distribution of the income:

Total income from all sources	87,978 *yuan*
Agricultural tax	3,386 *yuan*
Production and running costs	21,427 *yuan*
Public accumulation fund	13,068 *yuan*
Income distributed to members	50,097 *yuan*

Nor is it all a question of paying tax to the state and selling grain to the state purchasing commission. The state itself in the same year gave a subsidy to Bright Star of 12,000 *yuan* to help pay teachers in the new Brigade secondary school. They also received help from groups sent out by the Department of Agriculture

A Chinese-made tractor and DDT spraying unit in use in a cotton field. Vast quantities of pesticides and fertilizers are needed in a land being intensively farmed, but China is still unable to produce all her own. Fertilization by treated human excreta is an important part of farming all over China

on technical matters such as the prevention and treatment of rice pests and improved methods of silkworm culture.

On the wider commune level, a picture of progress is equally evident. The commune operates a machine-manufacturing and repair factory, a brick-kiln, a lime-kiln, a special nursery for bringing on mulberry saplings whose leaves feed the silkworms, and a veterinary station. The Bright Star Brigade itself, only one of many in the commune, operates four electrically driven irrigation and drainage stations, a forest farm, three tractors and eight electric ploughs.

The public accumulation fund is an important buffer against natural disaster, and also a source from which communal projects are financed. In 1971, Chiaoli's fund stood at 70,000 *yuan*, yet over the years the team has been able to build new barns for grain, new rooms for silkworm cultivation, and to buy new threshers and water-pumps. All the fields have been levelled so that drainage and irrigation are simple. The village headman, who is also secretary of the local communist party, is on record as saying that the accumulation fund should not be built up at the expense of a yearly rise in personal income for team members. And in fact there is a government regulation to this effect.

The average per capita income in Chiaoli in 1971 was 198 *yuan* (1 *yuan* is equivalent to slightly under 50 U.S. cents or 21 pence). It is not a princely income by any standards, but, considering that the main food of the peasants is rice and that each person had 799·4 *jin* of grain distributed to him or her in 1971 (it was 629 in 1960), and that vegetables and seasonings and sauces and even some meat are all home produced,

The friable loess soil in many parts of north China is being stabilized by tree-planting and by the use of controlled irrigation to allow the growth of crops and of cover-crops in areas where erosion was the perennial problem

then income is necessary only for clothing and other things such as saving up to buy a bicycle, a sewing-machine, new utensils or small luxuries. Cash income was 71 *yuan* in 1958, the year of the commune's formation, 132 *yuan* in 1965 just before the Cultural Revolution, and 198 in 1971. About 70 per cent of the families of Chiaoli have savings-bank accounts. With typical Chinese sagacity they quote the old proverb: "When there's water in the big river, the small streams will be full too." And by this they mean that when the state and the production team are better off, the life of the members also improves.

The picture of China's communes is one of a bewildering variety of styles and ideas—all in operation, shifting as experience and conclusions dictate best. No two communes are alike—for the simple reason that no two areas of farmland, plus townships and villages, plus industries, are alike either in their problems or in their geography. The tremendous advantage of the commune system is its flexibility, and on another plane its strength must lie in the ready participation of the vast majority of the people. In a population the size of that of China it would be incredible if there were not a proportion of dissident minds, or simply of people who are by nature nonconforming. Life is hardly comfortable for them in China because they are in a tiny minority within an organization that has the assent of the vast majority. One of Mao's statements, about the time when the Revolutionary forces were taking over all China, simultaneously points the way ahead and warns of its difficulties: "The serious problem," he said, "is the education of the peasantry."

At Liberation perhaps less than a quarter of the peasant population was literate. Centuries of grinding exploitation by the landlords, of extortions by sporadic warlord armies, and of the lassitude that comes of hopelessness and poverty and despair—these were the legacy of the bright new government in 1949. And these were the conditions of over 600 million farmers in the land. "Before Liberation," says the headman of Chiaoli village, "I farmed five *mu* of land and had to borrow at exorbitant rates of interest to tide the family over the winters." He now likens his condition to the bamboo shoots that sprout after the rain. "In my family of six, my son, my daughter-in-law and I are working in the team. My wife takes care of the house, and two grandsons are at school. Last year our income was 1,100 *yuan*, 650 *yuan* in cash and 5,200 *jin* of grain, and also oil, silk batting for padded clothing, and other produce." The family sideline produced 200 *yuan* from the sale of "three fat pigs to the state. We had new clothes for everyone and

An irrigation station at Kwanshan. Note the locally constructed pylons for the power lines, and people fishing in the spill waters

bought some furniture. My son purchased a seventeen-jewel Shanghai-brand wristwatch."

While he is not unusual in Chiaoli, it must be remembered that in "the land of fish and rice" the conditions of the commune members are a shade better than those of some communes whose land is less fertile, whose products are not abundant because of natural hazards related to the terrain. But the picture of the headman's family in 1971 is probably not very far above the average.

The immense variety of China's geography, climate, soils and what can be grown or reared on them, the huge problems of irrigating certain regions that are potentially fertile but lack water, and of course the lingering conservatism of many peasants (especially the older ones)—all these factors explain the wide variations to be seen in the communes. There are communes whose main income comes from bananas or from papayas, and there are communes in which the main work is forestry; there are pastoral communes whose members settled down from nomadism only a decade ago and whose flocks are mostly yaks and sheep. Obviously not all communes produce the same income for their members, the same standard of living. The yield of cash crops, such as vegetables, on communes near the great cities produces what seems a rather high personal income for their members. But such communes generally do not grow grain, and this staple food has to be bought by the members out of cash income.

There are hazards in any kind of farming, even in the most highly mechanized and best-run farms of the world, and China is far from being an exception. While superhuman efforts by both the state and the communes themselves have removed the risk of massive flood and drought disasters, which in the past have killed up to several million people in a year, not all hazards can be avoided. It will require many more years of canal-digging, dam-building and electrification before the danger from flood and drought is really a thing of the past. It will take many more years—to choose but one other problem—before China can afford or make as much fertilizer as is used on farmland in such countries as Japan. And without these fertilizers for the present, the highest yields of crops are extremely hard to obtain, in some areas quite impossible.

Echoes from the past

Part of the meaning of Mao's statement on the problem of educating the peasants lies in the outlook that is ingrained in people whose very

Opposite above: these laboriously built and meticulously maintained terraces are the sole way of farming steep hills. The method is not only Chinese but goes back thousands of years in East Asia

Opposite below: against the distinctive karst landscape of Kweilin in southern China, fishermen still use the traditional methods of dazzling lights and diving cormorants to make their catch

Household chores in Taichai Brigade. Behind, maize cores are stacked for firewood. The bamboo fencing is to keep chickens away from the plants

Mao Tse-tung and the then President, Liu Shao-ch'i, standing on the balcony of T'ien An Men (the Gate of Heavenly Peace) at the National Day Parade of 1963. The parades have recently been dropped and Liu has long disappeared in disgrace

existence has for so long depended on making a little extra money on every available opportunity and by almost any means. The necessity to do so has now been removed, but the instinct survives. This instinct, fostered by elements which, often unconsciously, wanted some holding back in socialist development and a return to "capitalist" ways of thought—meaning individual and private gain—was personified in Liu Shao-ch'i, President of the Republic until his removal in 1968. The process is one of extreme complexity that has been simplified and hung like a necklace of skulls round the neck of Liu and others. In this way it is more readily grasped by people with little formal education and less experience. The Cultural Revolution that swept through China in the late 1960s, rather like the Moslem holy war of old through the Middle East but with extremely little bloodshed, was considered a cleansing fire that incinerated those "evil weeds", as the Chinese say, growing like upstarts in the even fields of socialist rice. It is apparent, at any rate in the countryside, that the weeds were largely eradicated.

What the peasants have done to the land of China in the twenty years since the Revolution will strike the traveller returning to the country after that lapse of time as little short of miraculous. China is China—the strange sugar-loaf protuberances of the mountains of Kweilin still rise amid mists from flat grey sheets of water. The misty gorges of the Yangtze are still there, reminding one of a thousand poems, of trackers' songs when they still hauled the boats by main force against the treacherous currents. The man-made landscape of the loess hills in the middle reaches of the Yellow River, where the terraced fields reach to the tops of the hills in what look like a geographer's contour lines; the vast plains teeming with people still mostly clad in blue and black, still carrying the implements they have carried for a thousand and more years—these remain. China is China, and these things are still there. But just take a walk through any village and recall the stench there used to be, the dense clouds of flies through which one beat one's way, the diseased victims of dietary deficiencies, the children with the bloated bellies of undernourishment. Without painting a picture of paradise, it is safe to say that the traveller will not find these things any more. The immemorial, charming picture of a land embroidered with tiny patches of intensely cultivated fields—that, too, has utterly disappeared in favour of a more international-looking pattern of long abundant acres of rice, of wheat and maize in the north, and of horizons feathered with fine thin lines of saplings newly planted in their green millions. Many an ancient swamp populated by swarms of mosquito larvae has now disappeared—some local hill will have been removed in small baskets by the peasants and poured into the area after it had been thoroughly drained by the cutting of canals. The river you may have known, meandering peacefully for miles through the sallow swags of its overflow areas (where it was pointless to sow a crop for fear it would be swept away), now runs clear in a new straightened channel, and the land right to its very banks is planted with crops. Everywhere you see little power lines and telephone wires that hardly add beauty to the scene but certainly add communication to what was a series of forgotten little human backwaters. Everywhere there is, near or far, the small hum of some little motor pumping water up, or out, or in. And everywhere there are bicycles, hundreds and hundreds of people on bicycles. There is no use regretting the sweet, quaint, medieval look of China. It has gone. For most Chinese peasants it was far from sweet, and its medieval quaintness was only pleasant to the traveller's eye. The transformation in the Chinese countryside is after all no greater than that which occurred in England or in Europe between the reigns of Elizabeth I and Victoria. The only difference is that in China the scene has changed in twenty instead of four hundred years, and we have seen it with our own eyes.

Basically it is the aspirations of those millions of peasants that are changing the countryside. The Revolution has unleashed a tremendous reservoir of energy and ideas, which in China never had a chance before to set to work on a big scale. There are various contributing factors besides the actual communal farming processes. One of these is the emancipation of women. Instead of paying wages or grain to the head of a family, the communes pay them to the actual person who did the work. The wages and grain earned by a woman are hers and not her husband's and not her father-in-law's, as before. She cannot be forced into a marriage and no one may sell her children as used to happen in days of starvation. Marriages are by the wish of the man and girl involved, although the state officially frowns on wedlock until both of the partners are in their twenties.

A combination of education and experience has now taken firm root in the minds of Chinese peasants, making it quite obvious to women that the change in their status is good. And everyone realizes that only by the methods that have come into general currency could their backward state of twenty years ago have been altered in the way it has. If there is little time for the more frivolous things of life on the communes of China, we have to recall that in the past there was not the slightest hope for the vast majority of safety from the arbitrary strike of starvation, from unchecked disease and a life of poverty. It is quite unreal to compare the villages and villagers of China today with their counterparts in Europe or the United States. It would be more historically accurate to compare them in material terms with villages and villagers of Europe in the early 19th century. In this way we may find that comparison favours the condition and life of the Chinese country family today.

From 1937 to 1947 Mao Tse-tung headed a Communist government at Yenan in Shansi province. During that time he lived, like most of the people, in caves in the hillside. These cave houses are still used—they are warm in winter and cool in summer

CHAPTER TWO

POLITICS AND GOVERNMENT

Many times during the grand sweep of Chinese history power has been seized and dynastic government has been set up by men of very humble origin. Indeed, it is one of the virtues of Chinese history that, apart from the imperial house, few noble families continued to be noble for more than a couple of generations or so. The Ming dynasty, founded by a peasant who had turned monk to avoid starvation, is an example of this seizure of power by a man of the people. Another, more revealing in its way, is the founding of the Han dynasty over two thousand years ago. Liu Pang, together with his friends Hsiao Ho and Fan K'uai, were ordinary men who exploited and succeeded in focusing a mass revolutionary tendency of their time, overthrew the former ruling feudal nobility, and seized state power for themselves.

It could be said that Mao Tse-tung and his friends Chu Teh and Chou En-lai did the same thing in exploiting an already smouldering unrest among the peasants at the appalling conditions in China. Then they focused that unrest within the framework of their brand of Marxist-Leninist philosophy, overthrew the Kuomintang warlord regime, and seized power in the name of the people at large.

At this point the analogy abruptly and revealingly ends. In the Han and all other usurptions of state power, the peasants or others of extremely humble origin who achieved that power always, it seems almost automatically, enlisted the services of the establishment Confucian scholars of the mandarinate and the landlords in order to govern. Thus they ensured, with the inevitability of sleepwalkers heading for a cliff, their own downfall in the sense that power was sooner or later taken from them and fell into the hands of those who had always previously had it. The familiar old line-up of emperor, Confucian scholar-mandarins and landlords, forming a class opposed to the people at large, just continued as before.

With the Communists, however, an entirely new idea entered Chinese political philosophy for the first time. Instead of soliciting the aid of the former administrative personnel, Mao, in assuming power, deprived the scholar-mandarinate and the landlord classes of all power. The old story could never again be repeated, and a highly unclassical break occurred in that long scroll of Chinese history. For the first time, the governing body and the mass of the governed have no intervening filter, distorting mirror, barrier—it might be called many things—of bureaucracy. The old Chinese saying; *p'u yi chiang hsiang*, meaning approximately "peasant-smock

Schoolchildren in the countryside in South China marching like boy scouts with a red flag and portrait of Mao. They belong to the Young Pioneers—the red necktie being their basic uniform requirement. The outsize badges of Mao are now out of fashion

41

generals and prime ministers", applied as it was to the first rulers of the Han dynasty, is in fact a neat characterization of the top Chinese leadership today. The interesting events centring on the attempt of Liu Shao-ch'i and his followers (the "capitalist-roaders" as the Chinese call them) to wriggle into positions of supreme authority by means of encouraging the rebirth of an intervening bourgeois bureaucratic class, have been taken by the Chinese as another lesson not to relax the class struggle for an instant. For the meaning of Liu Shao-ch'i's policies and the tendencies of his followers lay really in the area of an attempt by the scholar-landlord classes and sympathizers to creep back into power.

Establishing the Constitution

The Constitution of China was adopted in 1954 by the National People's Congress meeting in Peking. To do this sounds a simple enough procedure, but it was not. During the years between the Revolution in 1949 and the calling of that Congress, its members had to be elected from the bottom upward by popular vote. That also sounds simple enough—but in China no such procedure had ever occurred before. The first step was to take a census, which was about the only step in the process that was not unfamiliar. It was no mean task in the early fifties, in a country so populous and so recently emerged from administrative and social chaos. But the Chinese have a long history of census-taking, the first recorded instance dating back before the 8th century.

The other steps—electing representatives from the masses, and those representatives in turn electing their choice, and so on up to the member stage—also took long and

provided the people at large with their early experience in democratic choice of leaders and representatives.

The document that emerged, approved by the Congress as the Constitution, contains 106 articles recorded in direct and simple language and is divided into four sections: general principles; the state structure; fundamental rights and duties of citizens; national flag, national emblem, capital. The flag is plain red with five yellow stars. The national emblem shows the Gate of Heavenly Peace (once the front gate of the imperial palaces) framed in ears of grain with a cogwheel at the

At the first National Games held in Peking in September 1959 in the newly completed Workers' Stadium. Left to right: Vice-Premier Ho Lung; Lin Piao (newly appointed Minister of Defence); Premier Chou En-lai; Chu Teh, Vice-Chairman of the People's Republic; Chairman Mao; Liu Shao-ch'i, Chairman of the Standing Committee of the First National People's Congress

base—a fairly neat symbol of authority, the economic base of agriculture, and the importance attached to building up industry.

Rights and duties of citizens are spelled out in nineteen articles. Seen through Chinese eyes and in the light of the long past when there were only the duties of obedience to the head of the family and to all men in established positions of authority, and when there were no very clear rights at all except those that wealth and power might confer on the few, these articles must have come as an eye-opener to the majority of people. But in fact to a Western audience there is nothing at all unusual in them. All citizens are equal before the law. Everyone over eighteen, regardless of sex, race, occupation, origin, education, or property status, may vote.

After two thousand years when the ordinary man in China had no rights except those recognized by some local magistrate in his *yamen* in the case of an otherwise irreconcilable dispute, and when the ordinary woman had no legal right to anything at all, this statement of equality made a clean break with the autocratic and male-centred past. The former "coolie", or hired

43

Premier Chou En-lai. Appointed to that office in 1954 by the National Congress, he has held the position ever since. He is one of the few Chinese leaders who speaks English and French and has lived in the West. A subtle and adaptable diplomat

The national flag of the People's Republic of China. The red ground, apart from being the colour of socialism, is also a traditionally lucky colour in China

hand, illiterate and depressed by a lifetime of the crudest exploitation similar to that of the worst period in the Industrial Revolution in Britain, hardly knew what to think. He was bewildered and it took time for him to realize the real meaning of his rights. The same was true of women whose subjugation was complete until old age lent a respectworthy position in the house. The deeply rooted pattern of obedience is hard to eradicate, and it took immense educational efforts on a national and also a personal level to convince those whose part in making the Revolution had not been active that they ought to use those rights. In the cities the task was generally greater than in the countryside where the peasants on the whole reacted swiftly and incisively, seizing their new-found powers. Already, before the Constitution was passed, they had dispossessed the landlords who had formerly dispossessed them.

The Constitution guarantees freedom from arbitrary arrest, the right to work and to improvement in general working conditions, the right to leisure and education for all, assistance to old and disabled persons, and the protection of marriage and the family. Duties include principally paying taxes, defending the country and military service.

Under the section headed general principles, the People's Republic is declared to be a people's democratic state led by the working class and based on an alliance of workers and peasants. All power belongs to the people, and they exercise it through the local People's Congresses elected by them, which in turn elect the National People's Congress. The concept of democratic centralism is laid down—meaning, in the words of Mao Tse-tung; "centralization on a democratic basis, and at the same time . . . democracy under centralized direction. This system alone can give expression to broad democracy by investing supreme power in the various grades of the people's congresses; at the same time it permits state affairs to be managed in a centralized manner . . ." Another writer has called it, "The bottom influencing the top while the top digests and interprets, returning messages to the bottom, and at the same time carrying out centralized functions."

China today. The population of each province is given in millions. Peking and Shanghai are politically separate from their provinces

Minorities

There are over 40 million people living in China, whose languages, ethnic origin and ways of life are non-Chinese—the National Minorities. Under the Constitution they were given for the first time equal status with the Chinese. In fact from early days in the revolutionary process such minorities were helped by the Communists. Their lot was a hard one, driven as they had been into the most inhospitable parts of China and forced to make a living as best they could. Now they are encouraged to send their brightest members to the special institutes and schools established all over China, where they learn the Chinese language and how to improve their own crafts and agriculture.

It was interesting and impressive in the 1950s to spend some weeks in such minority areas with Chinese cadres and others who were bringing medical assistance, training people in agricultural and other techniques, and at the same time conquering their own "great Han chauvinism", as they themselves were calling the former hostile and despising attitude of Chinese to these non-Chinese citizens. The problems in this programme varied. In some regions, such as south-west Yunnan, you could see how a fairly advanced minority people such as the Tai—literate and skilled agriculturists who had lived in a state of semi-slavery—quickly advanced, while in the neighbouring hills a quite primitive people not far beyond the Stone Age and primitive communism, practising pantheism, were taking much longer to move away from the state of mind which that stage of social evolution implies. The process was being carried through with great care by Chinese who were mostly young and had learned the several local languages. In this field of human activity, as in others, the Constitution was no mere formal document, rather a brief for action.

The Constitution also ensures that the means of production shall belong to the people in a socialist manner, leading to eventual transition to Communism. It gives the right to own savings, to own a house, and inherit private property, and it is amazing, considering the comparatively low cash earnings of the Chinese even today, how many people will tell you they have a savings account with the state bank.

The section on state structure defines the way in which the supreme organ of authority, the National People's Congress, is elected from the bottom up, and it goes on to enumerate its functions. Among these are important ones—to elect the Chairman and Vice-Chairman of the People's Republic, and to decide on a Premier of a State Council which it is empowered to set up on recommendations from that Premier. It also has the power to remove the members from office. The National People's Congress also elects a standing committee to supervise the work of the State Council and to attend to many other day-to-day matters. One highly interesting fact is that the "electoral units"—the smaller units all over the country that have sent deputies to the National People's Congress—have the power to replace them at any time.

So much for the theory of government. But what is it actually all about? Obviously neither the Revolution nor the Constitution caused great joy among the rich and the bourgeoisie. Neither was intended

Front-of-house posters at a cinema in Hangchow. On the left a feature film The Fen River Flows Forever. *This deals with the taming of the formerly menacing flooding of a river in Shansi province. On the right is* Number One Enemy of the People —*a documentary on American imperialism. The crowd, however, seem more interested in the photographer and a still rare foreigner with his camera and paper umbrella*

to do so. Both Revolution and Constitution place the value of life in China on work and achievement as having more meaning and giving not only more satisfaction but more equality to everyone than the struggle for money as an end. For the Chinese—a race formerly teetering on the verge of starvation and with a very small wealthy class and a small bourgeoisie—the Constitution and its effect as law meant the beginning of a new look at life. The Constitution is really the codification of the Revolution's aims.

To make it work is quite another matter. No one in his right mind supposes it is possible to alter entirely the outlook of most people who are already middle aged when they come up against a series of new ideas. The experiences of half a lifetime in another kind of society lay down certain pathways in the conscious and unconscious mind that can only with extreme difficulty be diverted. And at the same time, new pathways laid down at that age are generally less solidly founded. It is tacitly accepted that the eventual renewal of the population will take care of that problem in due time.

Continuing revolution

The only viable substitute for private profit, the mainspring of the capitalist system, is seen by the Chinese to be a society in which a continuing revolutionary enthusiasm for building a new way of life will make new men and women dedicated to the common good. And it is in connection with this particular idea that most Westerners begin to feel doubts about, and discomfort with the system, for it embodies ideas that are opposed to the capitalist outlook on life. The Chinese Marxist-Leninist view sounds on the face of things rather more like the Christian one, but in fact differs widely in that good is done not for any spiritual reason nor concept such as a god, but for the simple reason that it is said to be the best way of making a better life for everyone, the individual included. To be a Marxist revolutionary you have to be convinced of that, and in China it is remarkable how many are. But an energetic drive goes on via all the media all the time in China to instil this revolutionary outlook even deeper in each person.

The cadres, young men and women picked for their eagerness and political fitness to help, and also older people whose experience of the past led them long ago to reject the old system as they knew it, are the backbone of political education. But the relationship between them and their pupils—"the masses"—is ideally one of working together,

The notice says, "Philosophy meeting". This is a discussion group learning the sayings of Mao Tse-tung in Kunming, Yunnan province, in southwest China

At the 7th May Cadre School outside Peking, a political discussion meeting in progress. Most cadres who are sent to the 7th May schools are there to correct possible deviations in their attitude that might lead to a bureaucratic outlook

discovering depths in actual human work and personal relationships. The cadres have more skill in handling contradictions and in the method of resolving difficulties and differences. It is interesting to consider that in China today there are probably more people deeply imbued with the idea that life is lived for the common good than there ever were imbued with the true ideals of Christ at any time.

For a Westerner, to be in China today is a curious experience in many ways, not least in the feeling of extreme earnestness and honesty all around you. Sometimes people are so dedicated that they seem humourless but, the Chinese being Chinese, humour is never far off. And that human warmth that you find in the West, especially among old-fashioned country people, abounds everywhere in China.

The prudery of young Chinese people is often remarked on by Westerners. Certainly the outlets for licentious or riotous living no longer exist, but they never did for the poorer Chinese anyway. Part of this Western opinion is based on a misconception. The ordinary Chinese of pre-Revolutionary times who had not been forced into the gutter of life by poverty and starvation lived in conformity with the scheme of traditional virtues, which lent a fairly prudish air to life. The close

confinement of women to the house, the absence of boy and girl romances in a world of arranged marriages, the utter impossibility of a liaison between two people without discovery, and the whole system of a male-dominated, tradition-bound society, made prostitution and concubinage the only real outlets for men's wayward impulses. There were none at all for women.

saying, "The impossible is easy; miracles take a little longer". Kuo Mo-jo, President of the Academy of Sciences, wrote in 1963, when the results of the Russian withdrawal of help to China were becoming fully apparent, a poem which aptly sums up the mood in China today:

"Only among the cross-currents of this vast sea

In a cave house on a Yenan commune. Two faces of China — youth and age, renewal and the past. The old woman has lived most of her life in the old society, the young girl knows only the new

It is undoubtedly the unity of outlook that has been achieved in China today which makes it possible to move mountains, both literally and metaphorically, to get done just about anything that the will of the people wants to get done. Often when I was in China I recalled the

does the greatness of man become manifest.
The six hundred million,
having consolidated their unity,
hold fast to their beliefs.
When the sky falls, raise it;
When the world goes wrong, right it."

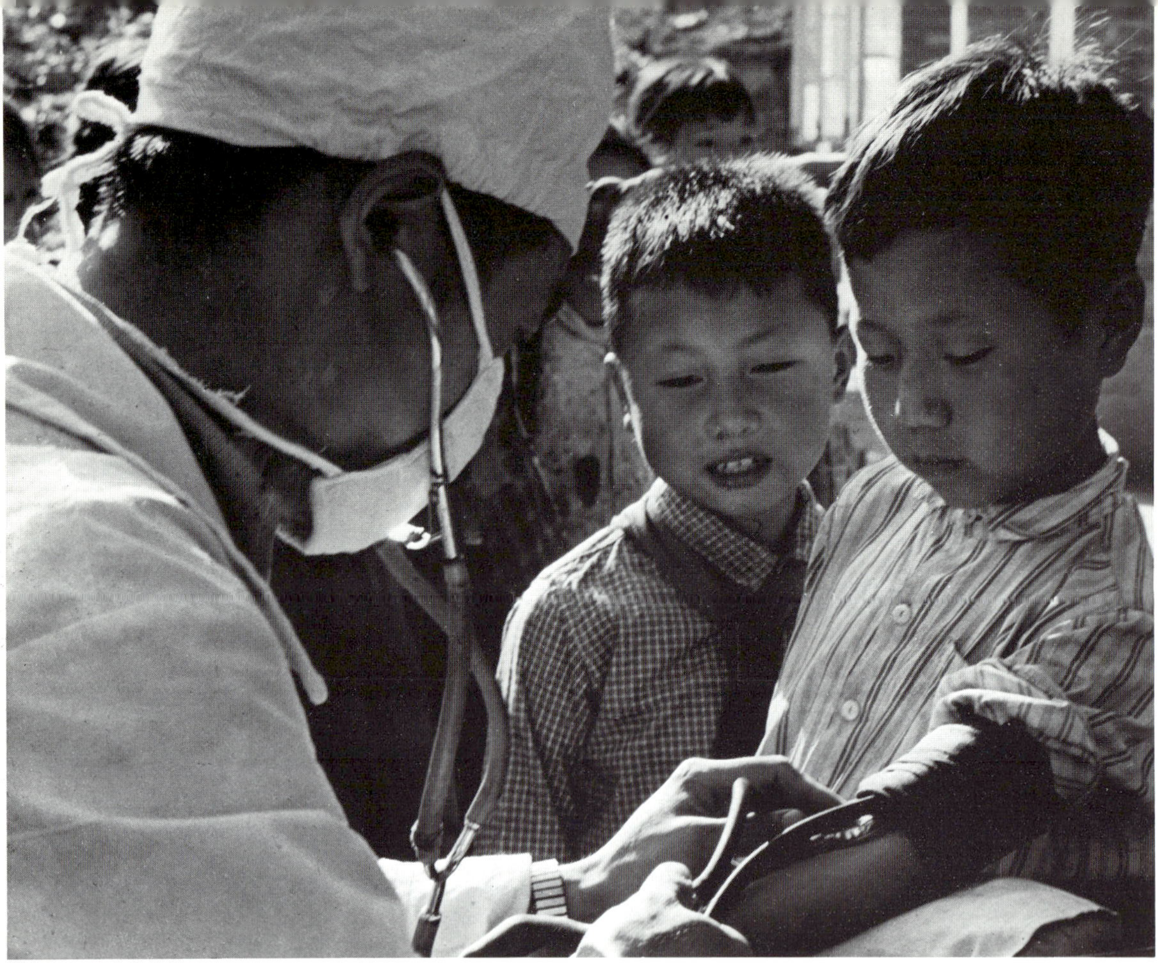

What now pleases and surprises the millions of ordinary Chinese is that they themselves have performed what no nation has ever done before in so short a time—many miracles that they can see for themselves and that no sour Western comments can deny. Any peasant or city-dweller old enough to recall the uncertainty of what tomorrow might bring, will now confirm that that uncertainty has gone. There is a roof for the family at a cheap rental, help in time of ill-health, food to eat, work to do, care for the aged if they need it, education for the children. To the affluent West these things are not very surprising, except, perhaps, in some areas such as cheap rents and adequate care for the aged. But, to put things in perspective, we have to consider that twenty years ago rather few Westerners lived on starvation's edge, rather few were ruthlessly exploited with no legal redress. We have to consider the matter to feel its bite. Not so the Chinese—they remember the lean years.

There are at least two main problems facing the government at this stage of the political and social change in China. One is the struggle against the remaining reactionary elements which continually tend to revert towards a bourgeois style of work and outlook, with its threat of incipient capitalism. This constitutes what the Chinese call an "antagonistic contradiction"—one between the people and their enemies. Another is the multiplicity of "non-antagonistic contradictions"—those among the people themselves. There are all shades of opinions about how to perform almost every single task—from the moving of a pigsty to staggering the

Ten minutes calisthenics several times a day are the rule in almost all institutions and groups in China. These are secondary school pupils

Above left: commune doctor in Chekiang province taking a young boy's blood pressure. Most communes have their own hospital and mobile health teams

Below left: breakfast near Taichai, northern China. The general standard of living and health has risen sharply since the Communists came to power. Starvation has been eradicated

working hours in a factory, from the finances of the production team's crèche to the technicalities of fertilizers. These things are debated at all levels, all over China, by hundreds of millions of people vitally concerned, and the answers arrived at are faithfully put into practice until the best method is discovered. China is a land of vast and myriad experiments—practically all of them proposed and worked out by people who, twenty years ago, had never heard of a fuse or such comparatively simple biochemical processes as the nitrogen cycle.

The Cultural Revolution

One of the most important sources of diverse opinions is of course the new youth that has never known the necessity of shutting its mouth in the presence of elders—even when they were plainly being stupid. The Chinese government and the Communist Party are evidently much aware of this boiling cauldron of drives. Its most important potential, perhaps, is that young people can produce exactly what the Marxist-Leninist-Maoist doctor ordered—a state of continuous revolution. Youth forces the pace, and in many ways that is what the government wants. The results do not affect only the youth of the country but the whole population.

The Cultural Revolution, which began with a "big character poster" attack by the students of Peking University in early June 1966 on the university head, may be viewed in this light. Soon the university head was dismissed, and even Peng Chen, Mayor of Peking, disappeared from that role. The reaction of the government was, as usual, cautious and delayed. Mao—with almost exhibitionist nonchalance it seemed—swam the Yangtze (or at least was seen to swim *in* the Yangtze), returning to Peking only at the end of July. But quite soon after that, in a dramatic gesture on 5th August, he put up his own *ta tse bao* (big character poster). It was entitled "Bombard the Headquarters!" and the message read:

"... leading comrades from the central down to local levels ... have enforced a bourgeois dictatorship and struck down the surging movement of the Great Cultural Revolution of the proletariat. They have stood facts on their heads and juggled black and white, encircled and suppressed the revolutionaries, stifled opinions differing from their own, imposed a white terror, and felt very pleased with themselves. How poisonous! ... Shouldn't this make one wide awake?"

Here indeed was what at first sight seems a very odd spectacle—the Chairman himself, the epitome

A party of workers celebrating their taking over of the factory during the Cultural Revolution. The slogan, "Red and Expert", meaning you must be a good Communist and also good at your job, is a fundamental in industry. There was much less industrial disruption during the Cultural Revolution than Western newspapers and so-called experts thought at the time. The main effect was the pruning of the dead wood of bureaucratic styles of thought and work

of governmental power, joining with the revolutionary student forces against the attitudes they discerned in that very government! What Mao was doing was to put his faith and his hope for the future in the youth of China as a force that, properly aroused and judiciously led, would get rid of the rightist opposition under Liu Shao-ch'i and his group. With many million big character posters, many million wordy battles, many a heroic Long March by mere teenagers of both sexes, and with not too much blood spilled in a three-year rampage, the youth of China, and Mao, won their battle. And nothing in China, from universities to the conduct of committees, from foreign policy to archaeology, will ever be quite the same again.

The events and conditions which riled the masses of Cultural Revolutionaries and against which they struggled, demonstrated to the young as well as to older people how authoritarianism and other tendencies could spring up, and how a class of people could begin behaving rather like the scholar-gentry of old —growing bureaucracy interested in itself, in the advancement of its members, and not in that of the masses. It was this growth, seen as a cancer in the body socialist, that was the real target of the Cultural Revolution. Such is the apprehension even now in Chinese minds, when for the moment the battle has been won, of some similar process recurring, that there is a detectable reluctance to elect heads, such as chairmen, of organizations. Vice-chairmen and deputies there are aplenty, running things with their committees and popular support. But chairmen seem still to be suspect in case, perhaps, those who would hold the office might abuse its powers.

Government now

At this point it seems essential to tackle the question of how China is actually governed today. Several things must be said at once, with the proviso that by the time these words appear in print they may have been contradicted by events.

As a result of the catharsis of the Cultural Revolution, several things happened in the sphere of how China is governed. One of these was the setting up of provincial Revolutionary Committees—an organization not envisaged in the Constitution. These seem to consist of cadres from the period before the Cultural Revolution, new revolutionary members who came to prominence

A poster of Mao in his character of the Great Helmsman, on a building in Peking

A schoolchild's drawing of the October First parade in Peking. The banner says, "Long Live Mao Tse-tung". The great military parades have been dropped in the last several years. T'ien An Men, the Gate of Heavenly Peace, forms the background

The Little Red Book consists of excerpts from the works of Mao and was originally put together for the army. Popular editions were published in 1966 and by now, next to the Bible, it is probably the most printed book in the world, running into several hundred million copies. Opposite: quotations being read during the Cultural Revolution

Production of the Little Red Book (the Thoughts of Mao) under a poster that reads, "When you sail the seas everything depends on the helmsman: this is the thought of Mao, November 29, 1967"

during that period, and army representatives (the army being the sole organization to remain intact—more or less—during the upheaval). There are, of course, the provincial Communist Party Committees as there always were, but these have been restructured during and since the Cultural Revolution and the 9th Party Congress. It seems that the chairman (if there is one) and some at least of the vice-chairmen of the Revolutionary Committees are generally the chairmen and possibly the vice-chairmen of the Party Committees also.

The situation is, however, not really as fluid as it might seem to the Westerner, accustomed as he is to cut-and-dried organs of government and representation. One thing that can be said of China today is that more discussion, decisions, discussion on decisions, and new decisions, taken in the light of the most recent discussions, take place at every level of activity, from the pigsty to the State Council, than in any other country in the world.

In effect, certain sections of the Constitution are in abeyance for the time being, otherwise how could People's Revolutionary Committees, which are not provided for in the original document, have been set up? But one may hazard a shrewd guess that the exchange of ideas up and down the echelons of government is probably more lively than ever.

The 10th National Congress of the Communist Party took place at long last in August 1973, confirming the disgrace of Liu Shao-ch'i and Mao's former successor-designate, Lin Piao. It may be regarded as a congress that attempted to consolidate in terms of approach and also in terms of personnel the lessons and the gains of the Cultural Revolution. The new party constitution was presented to the Congress by a comparatively young man whose meteoric rise seems to make him number three in China after Mao and Chou En-lai. He is Wang Hung-wen, until the Cultural Revolution an obscure official in a Shanghai textile mill. During the Party Congress, Chou En-lai remarked that the fourth National People's Congress would soon be convened, and after its completion both party and state will once more be in possession of new constitutions.

But we have not finished yet with the Cultural Revolution. The excesses of the movement have been taken up and inflated by the Western press at the expense of other aspects. Excesses there certainly were. Some material damage was caused, chiefly to old structures thought, often mistakenly, by the ardent young revolutionaries to be symbolic of all the worst things in the bureaucratic

The People's Liberation Army is concerned not only with defence but is also carefully instructed that part of its duties is to assist the civilian populace in every possible way. Insignia of rank in the PLA have now been abolished. This is a typical group of schoolchildren

elements against which they were fighting. Thousands of people whose thoughts and purposes were not at all with the Liu Shao-ch'i group, but who came to notice in one way or the other, were severely criticized and had a bad time. On the whole agricultural life was not badly disrupted. There was some interference with industry but not on the disastrous scale that the Western press seemed to think. All in all, the Western prophets of doom were proved wrong. Probably every single person in China had to think again about what his real intentions and his real opinions were—but that, doubtless, was all to the good. China emerged undoubtedly stronger internally, ideologically, than before.

One aspect of life in China that gained a renewed prominence was the perennial question of "class struggle". The Chinese view of "class" is, in political terms, at first sight peculiar. Your class is only partly what stratum of society your family used to belong to in the old days. Much more important is the picture you paint of yourself by your actions and words. There are plenty of instances of former "poor peasants" becoming bureaucratic wielders of power, just as there are numerous cases of former landlords' sons who are "honorary peasants". The struggle was and is not only against the former bourgeoisie as such, but against class enemies in the form of people whose attitudes and styles of thought and work show non-proletarian tendencies.

The new style of education both at school and university levels, which was necessitated by the Cultural Revolution's destruction of the former approach, lays strong emphasis on learning that is useful, as opposed to that which is merely of theoretical interest, and lays an equal emphasis on manual labour, on a better mix between theory and practice. This is true also of the activities of army personnel, who spend much time in factories and on communes. There are, to complete the picture, many cadres' schools where men and women, in positions in which they could easily get out of touch with the realities of life among the people whose welfare they look after in one way and another, are seconded to work in agriculture, small factories, and the like. The reason for all these activities is the same—class levelling, the rooting out of the tendency to form new bureaucracies and elitist groups.

It has been said that the special contribution of Mao Tse-tung to the theory of contradictions is that he showed how its universal law could be most effectively applied to down-to-earth practice. In doing so he has turned inside out the ancient Chinese concept of *yin-yang*. In place of the basic *yin-yang* statement that all things are composed of a balance of opposites and that normality consists of that perfect balance, the theory of contradictions states that all things contain contradictions—elements that struggle against one another. The way to progress is for one element to prevail over the other. In the end, to take a concrete example, capitalism and communism cannot really coexist peacefully, according to this theory. But to pursue a policy of peaceful coexistence is sound tactics. According to theory, the one will overcome the other in due course, because communism is seen as the logical way of life whose attractions will eventually win. Wars of liberation and internal revolts in other countries are seen by the Chinese as evidence of the strong tendency of the masses there to overthrow capitalist governments. Whatever the rights and wrongs of this approach, it is firmly held. The difficulties in understanding the theory of contradictions give rise to much misinterpretation of Chinese attitudes in other countries.

Thus China, in three turbulent years, was once more purified by the searching doctrines of Marx, Lenin and Mao. The remark of a woman on the commune at Chiaoli; "Now we know that the sharp class struggle will continue all through the building of socialism," echoes a general Chinese view.

Reading wall posters during the Cultural Revolution. The slogan at the top reads, "Defend Chairman Mao with your blood and your life". Posters were written by millions of people and acted as a means not only of denouncing people thought to be straying from the correct line, but also as an open forum for closely reasoned discussion on what the right line to take for the future might be. Posters like these all over China formed the largest and most prolonged public discussion ever held by the largest number of people in the history of the world

CHAPTER THREE

THE CITIES AND INDUSTRIALIZATION

A traveller returning to the West in the early 1960s, and rhapsodizing about the ancient and ineffable charms of Peking, was likely to be greeted by those who knew the city before the Revolution with scepticism, even with disbelief. The city they knew and loved, they would say, could hardly have survived the facelift it had received at the hands of the puritanical and iconoclastic Communist regime.

True, much had changed in Peking by that time, but there was still a lingering medieval fascination. Once within its sturdy walls, in sight of that vast sea of imperial yellow palace roofs, or wandering in the blank-walled little lanes called *hu tung* where in spring a sudden branch of blossom breaks here and there against a dark grey curl of roof, or in autumn the bright lemon leaves of the ginkgo trees carpet the dusty courts—once inside that Peking, the world outside seemed somehow a more ordinary place.

By the sixties, Peking had indeed been cleaned up. Long ago the hordes of diseased and half-starved beggars had been taken off the streets, the brothels and the opium dens had been closed. There used to be a saying that you always knew where officials lived, for the roads to their houses were paved. Even now, not all Peking streets are paved, but the 133 miles (214 kilometres) existing in 1949 have been augmented so that there are now almost 1,243 miles (2,000 kilometres) of paved road in the city. By the 1960s the charming, traffic-stopping old ceremonial arches, called *p'ai-lou*, had been removed and the traditional geomantic north–south axis of the city had been altered to run east–west along the huge new Ch'ang-an Avenue with a width which must be about twice that of the Champs-Elysées in Paris.

At that time the old walls, 40 feet (12 metres) high, 14 miles (22·5 kilometres) in circumference, punctuated by towering multi-storey gates, were still there, still reassuringly confining the city as they had done since the Yung-lo emperor built them to surround his new capital in 1420. You could take what still felt like a medieval walk, starting at Prospect Hill with its five romantic pavilions on the crest, just north of the Imperial Palaces, and go directly south on the geomantic course through the heart of those halls of former imperial power. All the great buildings of the palaces lie on this axis, among them the most perfect—T'ai Ho Tien, one of the largest wooden structures in the world. Here emperors of old held audience, embowered in the swirling mists of incense from huge bronze burners, and in mystery compounded of their unanswerability to anyone but

Foundry workers wearing protective clothing. There are steel foundries almost everywhere in China, mostly small. These are the result of the Great Leap Forward, during which the Chinese people at large learned (among other things unknown to a backward peasant people) that there is no great mystery about smelting iron and making low-grade steel. Many small steel foundries on communes make enough metal of high enough quality for most farming needs and for most repairs. The great steel complexes are situated in the northwest, and subsidiary ones, also quite large, at Wuhan on the Yangtze River, and elsewhere. China has in her own soil virtually all the other ores necessary to make all types of sophisticated steels—cobalt, chrome, manganese, and others

A winter view from a little way up Ch'ing-shan (Prospect Hill) north of the old Imperial Palace enclosure. The characters on the gateway read, "Imperial Palace Museum". It used to be, "Gate of Divine Military Prowess"

heaven, and the fact that all must kneel and knock their heads on the earth in the ritual of the kowtow. There, in the doorway of that gilded, painted, noble hall, standing before the acres of the great courtyard confronting it, you might still in the early 1960s get the feeling of vast power, in a vast land where that power had for so long been wielded in the same way. The medieval walk led south through the strong gate of the Meridian—Wumen—and out through the larger T'ien An Men, now the symbol of People's China, onward over the great new square flanked on either side by vast new buildings—the Museum complex and the Great Hall of the People. Before you lay Ch'ienmen, the front gate of Peking, dark and hieratic against the early morning yellow of the dusty sky, and through it, down that long straight road, eventually you would come to the Temple of Heaven.

Still, in the 1960s, to take that walk was to recapture a little of the dynastic feeling, and to recall how twice yearly it was this course that was taken by the emperor in his closed and sumptuous palanquin, or litter, as he was borne from the palace to make his personal kowtow to heaven, the only master he acknowledged.

Peking today

You can make the same journey today in a little over an hour's walking—but such is the change in the atmosphere of Peking, it is now hardly possible to feel in any immediate way the aura of past things surrounding you like golden spectres of former times. It is not merely that Peking is no longer a visually

romantic city, or that vast architectural and urban planning alterations have come about. It really has something to do with the people. Remote China, its inhabitants until so short a time ago still swaddled in their long past, its capital still very much the city of several hundred years ago—impressions such as these have all but completely vanished from Peking and from China as a whole. Peking, China, the people of China, have firmly turned the corner into the 20th century. The past, I was often told by people of all kinds, was in many ways a trap in which the ordinary person was caught. The laws of government and of conduct had remained the same yet the situation of China in the world had deeply changed. China had been quite unable to deal with the new world of technologically superior nations.

While Western visitors can hardly help feeling that something has been lost in the process of making a new and strong and fair-dealing China, the average Chinese (especially the younger people and those who suffered under the old regime) will quickly tell you how much they have gained. Romantic old Peking was probably not very different from romantic old Elizabethan London. Only the look of the buildings was good, the life of the ordinary man was not one you or I would like. Peking people can now catch a bus almost anywhere, a clean efficient service brings all parts of the city within reach at minimal fares. The walls and all the many gates except Ch'ienmen have gone, and new roads have pushed far out from the ancient enclave into vast new suburbs and even vaster industrial complexes. For Peking is an

Roofs of typical Peking hutung *houses, with modern buildings in the background*

Normal traffic on Ch'ang-an Avenue, Peking. The Gate of Heavenly Peace is at the top centre

example, one of many in China today, of a medieval city turning into an industrial one. Sian, the old T'ang capital, has also burst out of its walls and now makes textiles and most of China's millions of bicycles. In both these places the Communist government inherited cities planned and built centuries ago to serve a political and social structure, a way of life not remotely connected with the present. While it is sad to see them alter beyond recognition, we do not weep overmuch for Elizabethan London of which barely a trace remains. In China the changes that are taking place are comparable to those that have taken place between the reigns of the two Elizabeths in England: the difference is that they have happened in China within the span of one generation.

It is pointless to mourn the vanished past. After all, no one now under twenty years old remembers that past any more than European twenty-year-olds recall World War II. No ordinary Chinese regrets the destruction of many of the old courtyard houses in the narrow *hutungs*. Charming and friendly as they were even in their decrepitude, they were without modern sanitation and unsuited to life today. Hundreds of these houses were demolished to make way for the vast new square in front of T'ien An Men—a square that can hold over a million people—and for the Great Hall where an audience of 10,000 can be accommodated, and a banquet for 5,000 people given. The Hall and the Museum opposite are each almost a quarter of a mile long, and both were built in under one year for the tenth anniversary of the People's Republic in 1959. When I arrived in Peking for those celebrations and attended many gatherings in the Great Hall and its banqueting rooms, I remember my interpreter, who was a pretty young woman of about twenty, telling me how thousands of people went to help finish the interior decorations so that it would be ready in time. She herself had been down on her knees polishing parts of the acres of marble floors.

Like many other new buildings in Peking and elsewhere in China, the Hall and Museum have the old-fashioned, rather grandiose look of Russian buildings of the Stalin era. This is one of the unfortunate results of the influence of Russia in China before the Sino-Soviet split. China has little architecture of its own that can be adapted to modern needs—the typical Chinese roof supported by pillars, with walls that are not load-bearing, does not readily convert into a factory by enlargement, and cannot be adapted by vertical additions to make an apartment or office block. While it is highly questionable whether China really needs high-rise apartment blocks at all, she certainly requires factories and offices. But some solution other than the dead Russian architectural style would have been more suitable. The concrete multi-storey buildings of the early post-Liberation years, trimmed with magnificent Chinese-style roofs in green or golden tile, are hardly more likeable.

A whole range of these architectural banalities unfortunately lines the great new Ch'ang-an Avenue stretching from the east of the city past the new Peking hotel, the old T'ien An Men, the new square, the Palace of the Nationalities, the new post office, the new radio and television station, and many others. Passing straight across the city, the boulevard emerges from the old walled area of Peking into what used to be countryside and is now a very big suburb, with the enormous university complex to the north of

The Hall of Prayer for Harvests, the northern element in the Temple of Heaven, Peking. The emperor was borne on his palanquin over the elaborately carved marble ramp

Schoolchildren visiting the Imperial Palaces

it. The total floor area of new constructions built in and around Peking since 1949 is 50 million square metres (59 million square yards). As the Chinese say, two and a half old Pekings have been built. There are now seven million people in the city.

Despite the uninspired architecture, Peking is far from being a drab city. The very liveliness of its citizens would see to that, even if there were nothing else. Everyone in Peking, in China at large, works quite hard, and hours are long. But the Chinese are no less pleasure-loving than other people and take every opportunity to use the facilities they have nowadays for recreation of all kinds. And they love to go on outings in large groups. The idea that the Chinese are lovers of solitude, which has been conveyed to the world by Chinese paintings of isolated figures

Map of the city of Peking
Above left: soldiers in T'ien An Men Square
Below left: the Great Hall of the People, Peking
Below: on a bus in Peking. The services are frequent

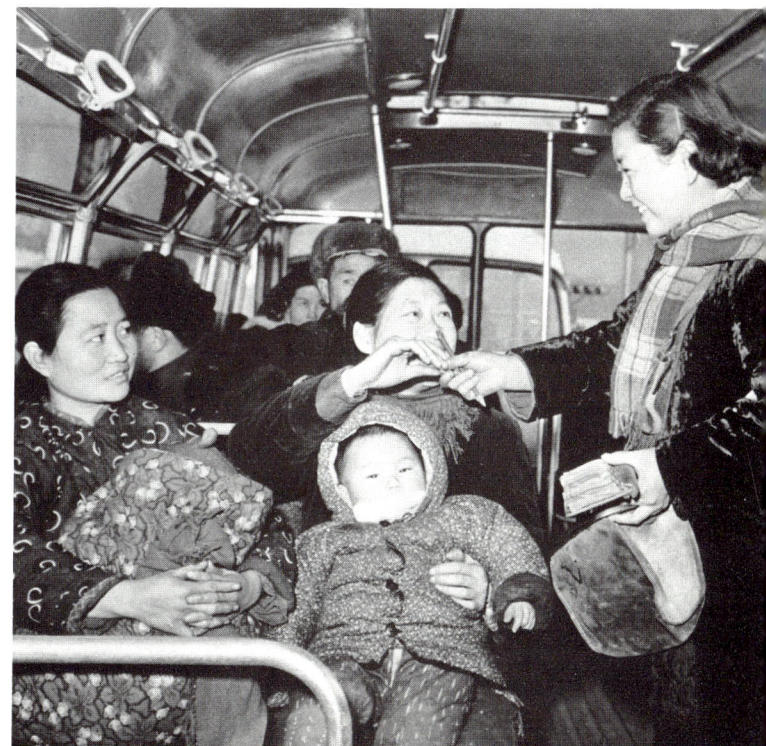

Families at the entry to the Summer Palace outside Peking — a favourite outing on days off. You can reach it by bus in under one hour. The slogan on the red cloth reads, "Work and save to build up the country". Another favourite picnic spot is the Great Wall north of Peking, a little farther away. The girl in the foreground with plaits and printed cotton shirt is wearing the normal summer clothes of Chinese girls today

in virgin landscapes of trees and mountains and scarves of morning mist, is misinformation. Only intellectuals in China ever had either the desire or the opportunity to be much alone. Whole schools, whole factories of hundreds, whole streets of neighbours, make up their minds to go to the Great Wall, take to their coaches and set off in a happily gregarious huddle of men, women and children. Once there, they swarm all over the Wall, lining up in big bunches to be photographed, and settling down to eat picnic meals in big clusters from which comes a buzz of talk. Any of these groups are quite likely to hold an impromptu political discussion meeting before returning happy and replete with simple enjoyment to the city.

I once went to the Great Wall north of Peking with several hundred geology students who were going to study the rock formations of the hills. When we arrived, they all scrambled up over the green hills, making a blue and red spotted effect, each spot a student with a scarlet scarf. It was a sunny, clear day in April. In the wind that cut over the parapet of the Wall from the north, your ears practically froze, while in the shelter of the southern side it was hot enough to take off jackets and scarves. The students all brought paper bags containing their lunch, and sat in circles to eat it together. One had a Chinese flute and played very well, marching up and down on the top of the Wall so that the sound carried far on the wind. It was a fine time. We all enjoyed the outing, and the students with their geologists' hammers, chipped lumps from various outcrops and (I suppose) learned something too.

Ch'ang-an Avenue in Peking. The pedicab loaded with goods is a fairly common sight, as are the Chinese-made bicycles

The entry gate to one of the Ming Tombs in the Western Hills outside Peking. The Chinese visit this beautiful park area, called the Thirteen Tombs because thirteen emperors are buried there. Some of the architecture is superb

Days off in China are staggered, so that any day in Peking you will find thousands of people strolling by the lake under the Dowager Empress's long, painted covered walks in the Summer Palace, and admiring her architectural fancies which, in the spring especially when the blossom is clustered on every blackbird-leg twig, look very pretty indeed. The near-by Ming tombs sheltered in the skirts of the Western Hills are a favourite place in the autumn when the trees turn russet and livid amid the browning scrub.

Peking, like all other places in China, nowadays gives the impression not only of bustle but of purpose. It is the latter aspect that is new. The reasons are not hard to find. Everyone has a job to do—there is no such thing as unemployment, and very little under-employment, I should imagine, in China. Outside what used to be the eastern wall of Peking, past that ancient observatory of curly astrolabes and quadrants set up when Peking was built, and refurbished by a great Jesuit scientist three hundred years ago, you come to the biggest industrial concentration in the capital.

Old Peking, say the Chinese today with disdain, was a "typical consumer city" implying that in reality it was a parasite on the body of workers and peasants. The situation has certainly changed. The Mao statement on the eve of the Liberation of Peking: "... only ... when consumer cities are transformed into producer cities can the people's political power be consolidated", has been followed carefully. In fact the value of the capital's industrial output in 1971 was 2·6 times that of 1965, and a staggering 93 times that of 1949. To the east, south and west of the city are mines and factories producing coal, steel, iron, machine tools, generators, diesel and other engines, motor vehicles, radio and semi-conductor parts, cotton yarn and piece goods, paper, and a host of other things such as synthetic yarns. There is, too, the huge Peking General Petrochemical Plant with an annual capacity to refine 2,500,000 tons of crude oil. It turns out gasoline, kerosene, diesel oil, lubricants, synthetic rubber, polystyrene and acetone. Truly, the West no longer has the chance to supply that traditional "oil for the lamps of China".

But perhaps in its way more impressive than these big plants are the hundreds and thousands of little "neighbourhood industries". These were started mainly by housewives in the Great Leap Forward in 1958, doing such chores as sewing for those who had no time, weaving, embroidering, making cardboard boxes. Now they have become very

Right: molten metal flowing from a blast furnace

Below: the Peking General Petrochemical Plant at night

Chinese bicycles, crowds, and a photographer's shop

professional little establishments and turn out simple farm machinery, cement, chemicals, radio components, and also process rare metals. One such place started by making water-buckets, and now makes blood-pressure gauges.

One of the delights of a stay in China is the absence of traffic, of urban pollution, and of the background of insistent noise to which we are accustomed in the West. There are no private vehicles in China. The trucks and cars you see are all state-owned. Everywhere are thousands of people on bicycles, and the tinkle of bicycle bells is always more noticeable than any other sound, even on huge Ch'ang-an Avenue in central Peking, or the Bund and Nanking Road in busy Shanghai. Traffic police, who are often women, have an easy job—there are no such things as traffic jams, and drivers who appear to be violating the rules of the road are quickly pulled up short and asked to reflect on what they did and to criticize their own behaviour. In the socialist society of China today, where the common welfare is put before the individual's whim, this is generally sufficient.

In the past twenty years, Peking has added many institutions and structures to its fabric, which never

existed before, while others have been enlarged and improved. Old Peking was without a planetarium. In line with the policy of widening the experience of the Chinese about the world at large, and in this case also the universe, a good one was built outside the north-east corner of the old city in the first ten years after the Revolution. It has the usual dome on whose interior is projected, by means of East German optical equipment, the appearance and movements of the heavenly bodies. But it also has various exhibitions of photographs, graphic reconstructions of the planets and other astronomical phenomena. There is, too, a telescope through which (at least in earlier years) wondering peasants peered at the fabled moon and were lectured on sunspot activity. To an historian this was in its way an ironic little scene, for it was only a few years after Galileo's *Star Messenger* dealing with the heliocentric theory was published in Italy in 1610 that Jesuits were teaching its message—that the earth revolves round the sun and not vice versa—in Peking. And, quite contrary to those Italian prelates who looked through Galileo's telescope and, while admitting what they saw, denied its truth, the Chinese were much more straightforward as they peered through the first telescope made in China not long after that.

Department stores are of course new to Peking, and nowadays each has its very extensive underground fall-out shelters running for many thousands of yards, often joining the systems of other organizations in the area. There is now in China accommodation for 80 per cent of the urban population in the city shelters. In Peking the underground railway, built a few years ago, runs from the 1959 railway station via the moat (long since dry) along the south wall of the old city past Ch'ienmen, turns north a little along the old western wall, and strikes out for a few miles into the big new suburbs on that side of the city. The line is not in regular use yet as a transportation system, but would

In a remote village in southwest Yunnan province, a girl of the Tai minority people using an old spinning wheel. The Tai people speak a language like that of Thailand, and also Chinese

double as a bomb-shelter if the need arose. Despite the great amount of digging activity in cities recently, the mood in Peking and Shanghai is now very relaxed—quite different from that during the Cultural Revolution.

The great sports stadium in the eastern suburbs holds 80,000 and is now over ten years old, as are the

The giant panda is native to Szechuan province and the adjacent Tibetan areas. In Peking they have been bred successfully in captivity. The panda lives on tender bamboo shoots and leaves

facilities of the Peking Gymnasium to the south-east, and several sports arenas.

There was a zoo in Peking before the Communists—a sorry place with a few mangy animals. The Peking guidebook, published in 1960, remarks with some disdain and unconscious humour that the "northern warlords, Japanese aggressors, and Kuomintang reactionaries stole and sabotaged, and . . . on the eve of Liberation the animal stock . . . had been reduced to a dozen monkeys, three old parrots, and a one-eyed ostrich." The authorities refurbished it soon after 1949 and restocked it with a wide variety of the animals we expect to find in any normal zoo. But of course the Chinese are fortunate in having a good supply of indigenous pandas from the borders of Szechuan province and the Tibetan region. Peking summers are very hot and humid—exactly the opposite of the ideal climate for pandas—and it is a familiar sight to see them sitting in the shade during the hot weather on large blocks of ice put there for their comfort.

In the years after 1949, an enormous new university was built to the west of the old city. The sheer numbers of students in each faculty was staggering—in the Iron and Steel Institute there were 4,200 students (30 per cent of them girls) by 1959, and this figure was about average for each of the several faculties. At that time, and increasingly so until the Cultural Revolution, the university was a city in itself. But during that upheaval great changes took place. The old competitive examination system to gain a university place was abandoned, since it was said to favour the children of higher officials and intellectuals. The new system requires each student to have completed primary or junior education at least, whereupon application must be made to the local Revolutionary Committee stating a preference for this or that subject. The prospective student's political awareness is then assessed by the committee—its assessment including a look at his or her knowledge of Marxist and Maoist philosophy, and the record of the minimum two years the student must have already worked at a factory or in the fields. After the committee's recommendation, the candidate still has to face a university committee which is the final arbiter.

It seems likely that the numbers of students have now dropped somewhat from the levels of the early sixties but, considering the size of China's population and her need for trained personnel, they will doubtless rise again. The universities, closed for about three years during the Cultural Revolution, have now reopened, and it seems that formal education—albeit greatly changed in its approach—has begun again. There is a great debate in China on the whole topic of how best to educate. Some time must elapse before precise statements can be made about its conclusions.

Shanghai

Shanghai, unlike Peking, is an example of an already industrialized city run by and for the Western powers before 1949, now turning into an even more intensely industrial place run by and for the Chinese. It was also, the Chinese will tell you, an example of what a festering sore a city could become under the rule of Westerners who were there only to exploit the people. Within such emotional statements there is a core of hard fact. A report in *The Times* of London in January 1945 recorded 800 deaths on one cold night in Shanghai when the freezing north wind swept over the city, forcing its homeless to huddle in corners of the local racetrack, in doorways, anywhere that offered a little shelter. Many were wrapped in old newspapers, their sole protection. It was a city of thousands of prostitutes, an alarming crime rate, opium dens by the hundred, child labour, and of human misery that had to be seen to be understood.

Today the total police force in Shanghai, a city of 10 million, numbers 1,000. There are still slums, but cleaned up, and the diseased, the prostitutes, the capitalists and the criminals, the Westerners and the starving are no longer a fact of Shanghai life. For a returning Westerner there is no bar in a city that housed not only the largest bar in the world but thousands of others,

A canal bordered by village streets in the village of Sha-chiao near Shao-hsing in the eastern part of Chekiang Province

and a Western face now causes a curious and friendly crowd to gather round. There are no bright lights, and the Bund—that street of hideous Western buildings of the twenties and thirties—has sprouted trees and beds of flowering shrubs. The racecourse is neatly divided into halves across the middle by a broad street, and its many acres are now a public park. Nanking Road is still the street of big shops, now department stores where you cannot find an item not made in China. The transformation of Shanghai is all but complete.

To understand what has happened in the last twenty years in China it is not enough to follow the transformation of a backward peasant society and its quite primitive agricultural methods into modern farming by quickly learning farmers; we have to take a look at industry. In the China of pre-1949, foreign business played the dominant role in the country's economy. All duties and taxes were controlled by the British, postal services were run by the French. All the Chinese banks together had less capital than the four big British banks in China. Half of the total coal production was in foreign hands, as was 45 per cent of the textile industry. Sixty per cent or more of China's trade was under the control of Britain and Japan in the 1930s. To add to this picture of what the Chinese call "semi-colonial status", was the ludicrous predicament of a huge country with over 74 per cent of its industry concentrated in Shanghai and Manchuria where it was later devastated by the Japanese, despoiled by the Russians, finished off by the Nationalists before it came into Communist hands. In the whole of the rest of China the remainder, slightly over 25 per cent, of her total industries were spread—if spread is the word for this scattering of small haphazard enterprises—at random.

Communist aims

On taking over, the new government was faced with a gigantic, a daunting task. A listing of the main sections of that task may help to make it clearer:

1. To eradicate the influence and control of foreign interests in favour of Chinese.
2. To expand all existing useful industrial production as fast as possible.
3. To find the correct balance between heavy and light industrial needs.
4. To find the correct balance between the priorities of agriculture and those of industry.
5. In setting up new industries and factories, to locate them logically in relation to raw materials, labour force, possible water and electricity supplies, etc.
6. To reorganize and to expand the communications network, and to relate it to a society that would sometime discard medieval agriculture as its sole economic foundation.

A temporary suspension bridge spanning the San Men Gorge on the middle Yellow River prior to the construction of the dam. The dam was being built with Russian aid, but when this was withdrawn the Chinese finished it themselves. With most of the hydro-electric station completed, the dam was finished not long behind schedule

In the industrial sector, even more so than in agriculture, at the beginning the prime factor was the question of education. It is hard for us to imagine the situation in China in 1949, when at least 70 per cent of the people were illiterate, and where probably nearer 90 per cent had never seen such elementary objects as light bulbs or petrol engines, and had not the slightest modern technical knowledge. At least down on the farms it was the same land that was to be worked with the same implements—only more efficiently. But in attempting to expand industry, it was a question quite often of utilizing people who had no knowledge at all of mechanical or electrical appliances—to whom a fuse was as much of a mystery as a battery light, for they had seen neither.

A knowledge of at least 1,200 Chinese characters is necessary to read a newspaper. Literacy drives were begun at once and in a surprisingly short time took effect. An official estimate in 1960 said that in the past decade in the countryside 110 million people up to the age of 40 had become literate. The figure in cities would be proportionately higher.

Initially, some industrial problems were solved with the co-operation of Russian technicians and the arrival of Russian hardware. Most Russian assistance was in the heavy industrial field and in large capital construction, and the early emphasis in China, as in Russia before, was on that sector at the expense of others. Without attempting to chart the course of the unhappy Sino-Russian marriage that broke up in the summer of 1960 with the sudden removal by Khrushchev of almost 1,400 experts from China and the stopping of most further aid, it is probably true to say that the divorce was a blessing in disguise. It saved China from the dangerous predominance of heavy industrialization, and it finally put the Chinese on their mettle. After the first stunning blow, the unfinished factories, the missing parts of huge and complex machines of which the blueprints had all been removed by the Russians—these things were gradually completed by the Chinese themselves. In the midst of the construction at San Men Sha of the biggest dam in China, for example, the Russians left, having supplied only a proportion of the huge and complicated turbines for the hydro-electric station, to be driven by the waters of the newly dammed Yellow River. With remarkably little delay, the Chinese made the remainder at Anshan in Manchuria and opened the dam and the power-station not far behind schedule.

New industries were begun at Wuhan on the Yangtze, and the first road and rail bridge spanning the river was built. Other heavy industry was set up in Inner Mon-

The first bridge over the Yangtze River, completed in time for the tenth anniversary of the Revolution in 1959. The upper deck carries motor traffic and the lower one is a double rail track. After thousands of years of separation by the unpredictable river, north and south China now communicate easily. Since this bridge was opened, another now spans the river at Nanking much farther upstream

Workers busy on high-tension power lines high above the canals and irrigated fields of a plain in Hunan province. The comparatively large extent of individual fields makes this landscape a new sight in China, where formerly all the fields were small, the land cut up by inheritances into tiny plots that made for poor utilization and poor crops

golia, and a new oil industry began in far Sinkiang.

In 1958, most large-scale industry was put under local control, and the Great Leap Forward was instigated. So much scorn has been poured on this epic surge in Chinese development that people in the West still imagine it was a total failure. The setting-up of thousands of little backyard blast-furnaces and smelting complexes to make pig-iron and low-grade steel certainly caused dislocation of transport, and all sorts of other anomalies. Much of the metal made by the peasants was useful only for making simple farm implements, although some steel was quite usable for other purposes. But at least half of the point of the Great Leap was that everyone was asked to contribute all the ideas they had for improving every aspect of every job. In the inundation of greater and lesser inventions and modifications that followed, together with the actual experience of making iron and steel (there were even grandmothers who learned how to wind armatures for electric motors!), millions of peasants just emerging from the arms of ancient superstitition learned that there was no mystery at all about industry. It was a dramatic step in education, in their rise from medieval backwardness. Ever since, the spirit and the lessons of the Great Leap have paid off in the increasing awareness, the resilience, the continuing inventiveness and self-confidence of people at large.

The Great Leap, with its slogan "Walking on two feet", meaning that economic improvement must be the product of both industrial and agricultural progress, made use of 500 million pairs of hands—many in activities that were quite new to them, many more striving in their own fields for greater production. In the year 1958, 93,000 miles (150,000 kilometres) of new roads were built, more than the total for the whole of the first Five Year Plan. Huge irrigation works were begun to combat flood and drought. The whole country was gripped by a fever of construction and improvisation. The result of the iron and steel drive was that permanent steel plants were set up in almost every province and, in spite of the comparative failure of the small backyard furnaces, those with a capacity of 13 to 19 cubic yards (10 to 30 cubic metres) helped the growth of steel output to rise from 5,350,000 to over 11 million tons in a year. Small coal-mines were developed everywhere that coal was to be found, and these managed to augment the total coal production by one quarter—270 million tons.

Time to take stock

Inevitably, the stresses and strains of such a concentrated, almost incredible, nation-wide effort began to appear, and with bad harvests caused more by natural disasters than the effects of the Great Leap, a time had obviously come for a pause, a rethinking of the whole national industrial picture. It appears to have been at this point that Liu Shao-ch'i and his faction gained the upper hand in formulating future policy—the policy that later required a Cultural Revolution to eradicate its effects. Just then Liu published a new edition of his book *Achieving Self-Perfection* (translated into English as *How to be a Good Communist*). Some of its contents are interesting in the light of what was to happen later. He condemns "those who think themselves the Marx and Lenin of China", and asks what turned out to be an ironic question: "Can we be certain that people of that kind will no longer rise to the head of our Party? No, we cannot." One of the fundamental problems in China (as the Chinese see it) is the fact that a new elite, a new ruling class, a new bureaucracy—some group dedicated more to its own interests than to those of the people at large—may at any time emerge and exert a broad influence before it can be checked. The "class struggle", which everyone in China tells you must always be waged with the utmost dedication, is their reaction to this recurrent threat and their protection against it. The threat consists of some form of "revisionism", such as that which the Chinese see in Russia where what is virtually a vast bourgeoisie has grown up, or some other form of reactionary attitude. The threat from Liu Shao-ch'i

No. 1 Printing and Dyeing Textile Mill in Sian near the middle Yellow River. Workers in industries where—as here in a steamy atmosphere—conditions are necessarily unpleasant, receive compensation in the form of extra rations and extra clothing. The textile industry in China is still not sufficiently developed to make enough cotton cloth to allow the lifting of rationing of this commodity. But everyone has sufficient clothes, and also warm clothing against the bitter cold of the central and north China winters

Socialist-realist-style poster showing heroic workers extolling the virtues of the Communist party. Pedicabs such as this one are on the way out. The scene is a Shanghai street

and his faction was that they opposed the continuing revolution and the constant struggle against class enemies, tending to a restoration of capitalism, and of the self-interest that is seen as the mainspring of the capitalist way of life.

On every level this struggle is still waged today, but never more intensely than during the Cultural Revolution. This vast eruption of political action was basically the result of the attitude of a growing class of people—from university professors to cadres in the factories and on the communes—that, since they had achieved on merit their positions of command, it was they alone who knew what was best to do. The whole concept of Maoist theory involves the idea "from the masses, to the masses". The opinions of the people as a whole are transmitted upward to the centralized organs, refined there, co-ordinated for further opinion, modification, action. Liu Shao-ch'i's line was essentially in conflict with this fundamental element of theory.

One other lesson of the Russian withdrawal and the Great Leap Forward is worth noting since it has an important influence on China's industrialization today. The Chinese realized that in a country of plentiful labour it is not only futile but utterly uneconomical to introduce immediately the fully automated, sophisticated processes that the developed, industrialized nations wish to sell. China, unlike other newly independent but backward countries, realized this in the late fifties, saved itself vast sums, and in the end obtained more benefit from the process of working things out for itself on the shop floor, in the drawing office, and in the seemingly interminable discussions among the workers themselves, than it could from ready-made hardware. In their own way the Chinese achieved results with people and improvization, results quite good enough for the present stage of their country's emergence from medievalism.

Any historian, probably any person with an interest in the stumbling progress of mankind from the chipped flint to the spacecraft, must find it intensely interesting to spend time in China now—to observe at first hand the development, the unfolding, of an industrial revolution. No one living is old enough to have attended the birth or watched the infancy of our own in the West, and after the Chinese one there will be no chance to observe another in a unified civilization. The Chinese industrial revolution is going fast—like a film projected at greater speed than was intended when it was shot. From the steam-engine to the placing of an object in orbit took several hundred years in the West. In China, partly, but only partly, on account of that Western process, the same order of achievement took a fraction of that span of time. One may usefully remember at this point the heady lead in science that the 16th-century Chinese had over a comparatively backward West.

Until the Communist Revolution in China, culture, intellectual life, were entirely literary concerns. The scientific attitude was foreign to scholars, and science as a respectable pursuit was scorned. Having said that, I should at once qualify it with a seeming contradiction—until the 17th century China was far ahead of the West in scientific invention and many aspects of technology. This is fact not fiction, attested by many an astonished and learned Western traveller of these times and before. How did this come about?

Chinese technology

Much of the wealth of technical knowledge was incidental to the researches of Taoist mystics looking for, among other things, a means of transmuting cinnabar (mercuric sulphide) into silver, just as Western alchemists searched for the Philosopher's Stone that would turn things to gold. And there were hosts of non-scholars who, in the course of ordinary work, became inventors and proto-scientists.

The list of Chinese inventions, many of them coming long before their equivalents in the West, is lengthy and curious, but a few will serve to show the scope of scientific achievement. Not unnaturally, in a land whose climate is often extreme and whose harvest has traditionally been dominated by the vagaries of two huge and many smaller turbulent rivers, all manner of hydraulic inventions are of great antiquity there. One of the great legendary "culture heroes" is Yü who is credited with the taming of the Yellow River—which, however, apparently

A scale model of an astronomical tower run by clockwork powered by a waterwheel. The original was constructed in A.D. 1090 by Su Sung in K'aifeng, Honan province. Its mechanism rotated an observational armillary sphere on top, and a celestial globe inside on the upper platform. Inside the tall doors a rotating pagoda-like structure showed the time in various small windows. The invention of the essential escapement was made first in China

got out of hand again after his time and was not finally tamed until a few years ago! But canals, locks, the art of dike-building on a grand scale, were early achievements. So also were gunpowder, paper and porcelain—the last two originating before the time of Christ. Paper appeared in the West about a thousand years later and porcelain not until the beginning of the 18th century. The compass, movable type for printing, watertight compartments in ships, a steam turbine—all were known and written about in considerable detail, but quite often inventions were then lost, sometimes due to the scholarly copyist who failed to understand what the text was about. More often, however, the literary attitude scorned inventions as trifles. A 17th-century Jesuit built for the emperor a small cart and a small paddle-boat, both driven by steam jet, and there, as imperial toys, the matter rested. The same Jesuit and his predecessor in Ming days had presented the emperor with fine French clocks, neither realizing that steam-power and clockwork were in fact old Chinese inventions. So was the rotary winnowing machine, a machine that was much in use, but the "south-pointing chariot", a vehicle whose wheels were so geared that, no matter how twisting the road, the hand of a figure on a pole always indicated south, remained a curiosity, an amusing whimsy.

All this technical brilliance was from the very beginning non-Establishment. There never was a famous scientist as such—no household name such as that of Archimedes or Darwin, except perhaps for the Great Yü. Learning was a matter for scholar-gentry who wrote, not ever for men who conducted anything like an experiment. That was left to those cranks and Taoists and incidental inquiring souls who happened to be made that way.

Standing back a little—as we now may after the Great Leap Forward, followed and preceded as it was by many lesser campaigns, and after the Cultural Revolution which has now been wound up—standing back, what has been achieved as a result of the interlocked processes of education and industrialization, of the introduction of scientific thought?

The Chinese will answer first of all with a volley of statistics, from which we may perhaps take just a few. Steel production has risen from its 1957 level, before the Great Leap, of 5·3 million tons to 10 million before the Cultural Revolution, and in 1971 stood at the astonishing figure of 21 million tons annually. Almost four times the length of railways that existed in 1949 is now in operation, and every province in China except Tibet can now be reached by rail. The irrational concentration of railways on the coast and in the north-east has been overcome. There are now over 375,000 miles (600,000 kilometres) of good roads in China, compared to 46,875 (75,000) in 1949, and these too have been constructed to serve a rational pattern of resources, industries and consumers. The length of inland waterways navigable by commercial boats has doubled in the same period. A regular postal service reaches virtually everyone in China. The petroleum output has risen 300 times in the past two decades, and the volume of retail sales is 600 per cent up on 1949. A question that will spring to anyone's mind at this point is: what can the Chinese buy, with what wages, and how much do things cost?

In the country, grain constitutes a large part of the peasant's "income" so his actual cash earnings are proportionately smaller than the city-dweller's. Variations are not

China's rapid industrialization has required millions of people to learn techniques and whole subjects that never before had a place in general schooling. Giant mechanisms such as this section of a turbine are made in China to Chinese designs. The list of important scientific inventions that are Chinese is quite long. Even such "obvious" mechanisms as the wheelbarrow were in use in China almost a thousand years before they appeared in the West. Cast iron, deep drilling, the iron chain suspension bridge, and porcelain, were all known in China a thousand years before Europe heard of them, as was paper and the magnetic compass using a lodestone spoon floating on water. The idea that scientific invention and discovery was the gift of the West to the East must be drastically revised in the light of modern knowledge

A postman delivering letters. In the country where one commune may extend for miles in all directions and include several dozen villages, townships and scattered industry, communications are important. Most communication is between commune headquarters and various brigades and units forming the commune, and between them and the headquarters. But of course people write to relatives and friends in other parts of the country — something quite new to the majority of Chinese

huge between one type of worker and the next, nor even between those in positions of great importance and those in lesser positions. Some recent examples given by Western travellers, which agree very well with official Chinese sources, will give a general picture of personal and family budgets in the cities.

The editor of one of Shanghai's main newspapers earns 70 *yuan* a month (about £14 or $35), while a skilled craftsman in a Shanghai jade factory gets more—in the region of 100 *yuan* (about £20 or $50). A man and his wife working in a Shanghai factory making rubber drive-belts for industrial machinery earn between them about £30 ($75) a month, and their rent is just over £1 ($2.50) for a two-room house. Rents in all cases are extremely low by Western standards. The ordinary family with two rooms and kitchen is likely to pay anything from 2 to 5 *yuan* a month—in other words up to about £1 ($2.50).

A pound of rice costs, according to grade, from 2 to 3 pence (5 to $7\frac{1}{2}$ cents), pork is about 18 pence (45 cents) per pound, cooking oil about 15 pence ($37\frac{1}{2}$ cents) a litre (2·2 pints). A pound of apples costs 8 to 9 pence (20 cents) and oranges are slightly dearer. A can of beef is under 30 pence ($75\frac{1}{2}$ cents) and one of fish cheaper. *Maotai* and various other Chinese spirits, which are of the potency of vodka and taste stronger, cost something under £1 ($2.50) per litre. Excellent restaurant meals with that soft-tasting, heated rice wine that goes so well with Chinese food are in the general region of 65 to 85 pence ($1.60 to $2.12).

You can buy a transistor radio for £4 ($10) and upward, depending on the size, while a bicycle can cost up to £30 ($75). Cotton clothing is still rationed, and a heavy padded winter jacket for the northern and central Chinese cold runs at £2.40 ($6) and up. A pair of leather shoes costs £2 ($5), but the canvas, rubber-soled shoes that most people wear are only 60 pence ($1.50) a pair.

The prices of grain, salt, coal, edible oils, cotton cloth and many other necessities have remained stable for two decades, and there have even been cuts in prices of medicines, which have fallen by 20 per cent. In the agricultural and industrial field the cost of chemical fertilizers, insecticides, diesel fuel and other commodities has fallen between one-third and two-thirds compared with that of 1950.

One pointer to the comparative stability and security of life for the Chinese both in cities and on the land is the fact that nearly everyone confesses to having some savings in the bank. The rate of interest on savings is 3 per cent per annum.

These savings may not be much, but they serve as occasion demands for the purchase of a sewing-machine, a new radio, a bicycle, household furniture, new suits of clothing, and for similar larger expenditures. China is far from being an affluent society, but when comparison is made between the conditions inherited by the régime in 1949 and those of today, it is not surprising that most Chinese find their lot a not unhappy one.

A recent official statement remarks: "The achievements we have made are great, but they are only the first steps in a long march. Ours is a developing country: the level of our economy, science and technology is not high, and the per capita output of steel is still quite low." The first heady years of what seemed then unimaginable success, have been tempered with the facts of experience, and that statement has the sober ring of facing up to realities.

A vegetable market. The variety and abundance of Chinese vegetables is astonishing; there are at least ten different types of cabbage alone. The numerous root vegetables range from ginger to turnips, while there are all manner of nuts and delicious bamboo shoots

CHAPTER FOUR

THE ARTS AND COMMUNICATION

When we think of Chinese art, we think of poetry, scroll-paintings, porcelain, and perhaps Chinese opera. The West has not had much of a chance to learn about the latter, and knows even less of the architecture and sculpture.

When a pre-Revolutionary Chinese considered his country's art, the subject that probably came first to his mind was calligraphy, allied to painting and followed by porcelain.

If you ask the Chinese today about Chinese art, they will probably begin by quoting from Mao Tsetung's *Talks at the Yenan Forum on Literature and Art*, "All our literature and art are for the masses of the people. . . ." Literature and art are "powerful weapons for uniting and educating the people and for attacking and destroying the enemy. . . . All the dark forces harming the masses of the people must be exposed and all the revolutionary struggles of the masses of the people must be extolled."

Once these words and their implications have been understood, much that is otherwise mystifying in the arts of China today becomes clear. It is rather obvious that the delicate and subtle art of calligraphy is unlikely to arouse much revolutionary fervour in the Chinese breast, and that the idealized nature of dreamy Chinese landscape-painting is not the kind of stuff to speed the plough in the drive for ever-increasing production. The verging-on-occult beauty of the masterpieces of Chinese porcelain does not, at this early stage in the process of revolution, find much of an echo among the factory workers of the new proletariat in their attempts to keep 800 million pairs of hands supplied with rice-bowls and 800 million backs adequately covered with at least one new suit of clothes per year.

The priorities in the arts of today's China may perhaps be listed with fair accuracy as these: graphic material of all kinds which shows people winning the battle for production and socialism, or that points out in realistic if highly dramatized terms the evils of the old society; stories and poems which tell in simple and direct words of the achievements of ordinary people in the struggle to overcome various personal or community defects in ideology or, in heroic terms, how they battled against natural disaster such as flood or drought, and won.

Chinese opera

Before the Revolution perhaps the most lively art form was the Chinese opera. Painting, sculpture and the real greatness of Chinese porcelain had long since degenerated for the

A modern painting of life on a commune. It may not be great art but it does show in a pleasing way many of the activities. The hills have been carefully terraced for cultivation and the peasants are planting them. The water of the river bears timber extracted from the forest, while two small pumps on the banks send water in pipes uphill to irrigate the crops. On the left, people have been cutting bamboo from the groves, while others are working and driving a truck and a tractor. In the building is what may be a generator driven by water-power from the river. Note the few traditionally shaped white clouds, top left, virtually the only element of the past in the picture

A fine example of tê-hua (blanc-de-chine) porcelain depicting Kuan-yin, the Goddess of Mercy

Paper-making by covering a fine rattan screen with liquid pulp, then allowing it to dry. Stacks of finished paper are on the right

most part into clever but uninspired imitation of old masterpieces. Opera has its roots far back in the Sung dynasty and even earlier. Its repertory stems from the Yüan when, under the Mongol heel, many a concealed satire was introduced. And in the Ming the medium was perfected. A cultured pre-1949 Chinese would not have included opera as an art—largely because it was a popular form. But art it was, and no mean form at that. Its stories were for the most part about emperors and high officials, intriguing generals and traitors, eunuchs, concubines and melting young women with the fluttering hands and profound coyness of the sheltered upper classes. The commoners in these operas were mostly soldiers, villagers, servants and grooms (very much the caste discovered in wooden and porcelain figurines in Han and T'ang tombs). Oddly enough they had at least half of the best lines and situations, for they were the comedians, providing the light-hearted buffoonery and relief from events of portentous magnitude.

The female parts were played by men—the last and greatest performer in this field being Mei Lan-fang. He was a man of great personal charm, unassuming and modest when you talked with him, obviously intelligent, with the alert eyes of one who misses little that is going on. In his sixties, he still gave magical performances in the part of a seventeen-year-old girl. The great scenes of the old operas had the authentic spellbinding quality that distinguishes all great art.

After the Revolution, these old operas were "cleaned up" and the offending scenes removed or rewritten. But in the 1960s a limited number of new operas emerged, dealing with revolutionary situations of only yesterday, when the Japanese occupation of China and the civil war between Nationalists and Communists were the issues of the day. The old operas vanished. Unlike the walls of Peking, they can and doubtless will be seen again in all their greatness when their contents are less touchy. In fact, it has recently become known that one or two of the old operas are soon to be staged again, in what form we must wait to discover.

The driving force behind the new operas was partly Chairman Mao's wife, Chiang Ch'ing, herself formerly an actress in Shanghai. She does not cut a very graceful personal figure, and the extreme vehemence of her ideological posture has at times been rather far-out. But doubtless the problem had to be tackled somehow, and she may have been the best person to do it.

There are five new operas: *The Red Lantern*, *Taking Tiger Mountain by Strategy* (not exactly a catchy title but reckoned by many to be the best opera after *The Red Lantern*), *Capturing White Tiger Mountain* (about Chinese volunteers in the Korean

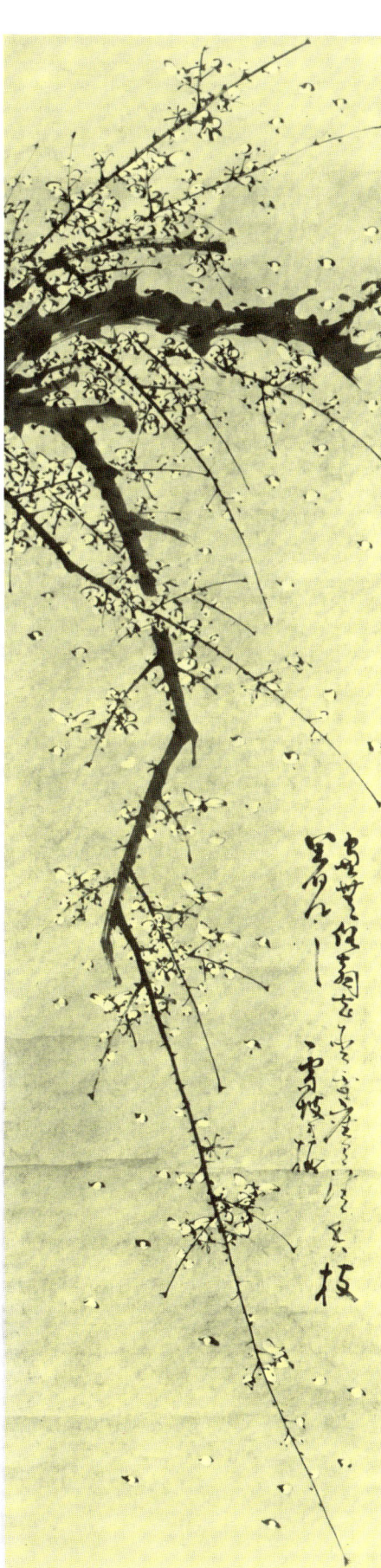

Traditional-style painting of a blossoming branch, on silk. The calligraphy at the right is a comment on the subject. Alongside the various types of socialist realism favoured in China, the use of brush and Chinese inks in the manner of this or that great painter of the past is still widespread. Probably, among a people whose writing is basically brush-drawn calligraphy (however much it may now be done with Chinese-made ballpoints), the traditional techniques of exploiting every possibility of the brush with ink on paper or silk will persist at least as long as the use of calligraphy. What is not *happening in China is the really creative use of the miraculously fine techniques of the brush*. To find this one has to go to Hong Kong where it is happening to some extent, and with remarkable results

War), *Shachiapang* (dealing with the 4th Army), and *On the Docks* (about a "hidden class enemy" among the dock workers in Shanghai).

The story of *The Red Lantern* is fairly typical of the new operas. Set on a cold winter's night during the war of resistance against the Japanese, it tells of the dangers encountered by a member of the Communist Party, Li, a railway signalman, and his daughter, Tiehmei, a pedlar, in their efforts to pass a vital message to the guerrillas fighting in the near-by mountains. The plot contains all the elements of melodrama—a hidden code, brutal Japanese police, a treacherous double-agent, torture and death; but in the end a victory despite all.

Even shorn of most of its political messages and heroic speeches and songs, the story has exciting possibilities for the stage or film. Even as presented on stage in China there are excellent tense scenes. But for a Westerner, the effect of the whole is too deeply heroic and idealized to be moving. As criticism, this is neither here nor there—the production is designed for Chinese, and Chinese audiences show every sign of liking it. The highly stylized groupings of the old opera are all there; the songs follow much the same old tunes and techniques of voice production characteristic of Chinese and no other operatic performances. The good wins out over the bad—however new the characters are to Chinese opera. And the message is one that—with the recent history of China in mind—is far from unreal to most of the audience.

As non-Chinese, lacking the particular history and experiences of the ordinary Chinese people in the last century or more, and especially in the past thirty or forty years, you and I are not likely to get the most out of the new Chinese operas. They are designed not only to entertain but, rather in the manner of the old morality play in Europe, also to

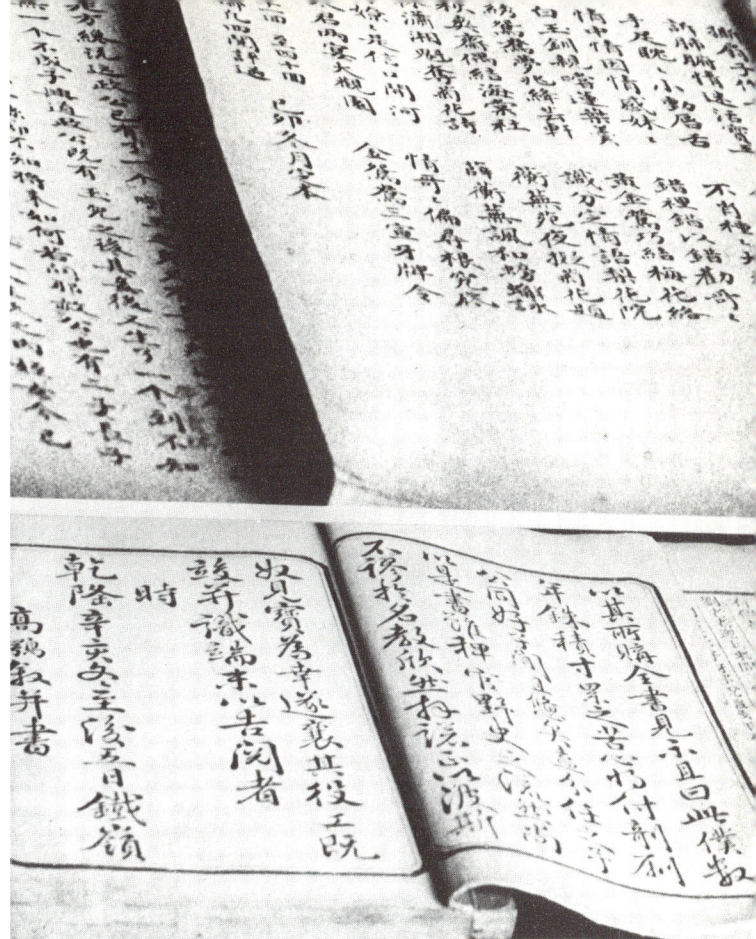

Examples of different styles of calligraphy in an exhibition commemorating the 200th anniversary of the death of the author Ts'ao Hsüeh-ch'in

Left: the art of woodblock printing is extremely old in China, but the approach to figure-drawing in this print is entirely foreign

Opposite: another modern painting in traditional style. The inscription reads, "Lushan. I went along the Yangtse River and climbed Lushan, then returned to Nanking to paint this picture. Ch'ien Sung-yen"

A giant poster showing Mao among workers

A scene from the traditional Chinese opera Mu Kwei-ying Takes Command, *dealing with a Sung dynasty woman general (right), played here by Mei Lan-fang, the most famous 20th-century male player of female leads, an actor and singer of great brilliance. Both characters are generals*

instruct, to edify, to raise the moral consciousness of the audience by reflecting situations more or less within the experience or grasp of all.

It is a truism that the realities of life in a country occupied by enemies are hard to imagine. Any Frenchman will recall the facts of occupation, any Englishman will find it difficult. He will more easily recall the efforts the English at that same time were making at home to win the war—the rationing of food, the astonishing togetherness of the people striving for one end, old ladies who never before dirtied their fingers doing wonders with pigs, children collecting every scrap of waste for the national war effort. The atmosphere in China is not unlike that in war-time England except that there is no enemy raining bombs on the country. The people have been united for the national good. It is in this somewhat intoxicating atmosphere that the operas have to be considered.

The old ramshackle town theatres with their cheerful dirt, attendants throwing hot wet towels to patrons along the rows, others serving snacks, and the general six-hour rowdiness of each performance, have gone. The new theatres are Western-style with proper lighting and curtains. The orchestra no longer sits on one side of the stage smoking cigarettes at less active moments, but has been consigned to the pit as in the West. And the performances no longer last six hours but something more like two. In the country, however, touring groups still set up in the villages of the communes and do a two- or three-night stand—or just one, where the audience is small. Although you no longer see small opera troupes walking along country roads pushing their props and costumes on handcarts from village to village, the same little companies do go to the same sort of places—but by bus.

Far more people now see operas and, to judge by experience of mass interest in other matters, far more people are soon going to make their opinions heard on the subject. In the end, the diet of undiluted heroism will be modified by the audience. This is one of the things to marvel at in China—the dogged resistance to various aspects of the new life, and the equally persistent clamour for other and better things. No amount of pleading or planning could finally get the peasants to eat all their meals in the canteens, so the canteens more or less folded up. And the new operas have been considerably modified since their first appearance. One, *On the Docks*, was such a flop that it disappeared until it had been virtually redone. Eventually the idealized realism of today's China in the arts will give way to something more profound.

Films in China

Oddly enough, since the Cultural Revolution no new feature films have appeared to add to the scanty number produced before it, and the recent films have followed the tradition of former years in being cinema versions of operas. The film medium as such is not really utilized. Its huge potential for persuasion, for turning emotions on and off, for telling dramatically and realistically almost any good story, has remained untapped. While there are plenty of fairly pedestrian but serviceable

Four scenes from the modern opera The Red Lantern. *The story deals with a railwayman, his mother and daughter, and their exploits during the Japanese occupation of China as they relay an important message in secret code to Communist guerrillas in the mountains*

A performance of The Red Detachment of Women. *The orchestra, using Western instruments, has been placed where it belongs in the West, instead of at the side of the stage*

Kindergarten children acting

documentaries on how canals were dug, irrigation expanded, houses built, factories rushed up in incredibly short periods of time, and the like, there is no great stirring story of a group of teenagers during the Cultural Revolution, who took the law into their own hands and sorted out the ideological mess they found around them. There are hundreds of such stories already recorded by the Chinese press, just waiting for the writers to write and the directors to direct. The absence of such films is striking, and the reasons obscure. Possibly the writers who could put such stories into dramatic form are inhibited by the uncertainty that always surrounds movements such as the Cultural Revolution. Already, a few years later, segments of events during those stirring years have been condemned as "left deviation"—going too far, in other words. And some of the very highly placed officials who went into political eclipse have re-emerged, a typical recent example being the rehabilitation of the disgraced Teng Hsiao-ping, once General Secretary of the Communist Party and a Vice-Chairman.

There is nothing new in the arts being used by the state or other organizations to communicate a message (commonly called by that loaded word "propaganda"). The history of Western literature, to look no farther afield, is full of it. In England we have Pope's political satires in poetry, Swift's in prose, Noel Coward's Establishment patriotism during World War II in that film with a simple and moving story of the navy, *In Which We Serve*. There are, too, the calculated posters of World War I—the finger pointing directly at the viewer with the injunction to serve his country—and the equally striking and somehow insidious ones of the last war

enjoining people not to talk incautiously. In China, however, such means are new. In pre-Revolution days there were not enough literate people, and rather few, apart from some town-dwellers, ever had much chance to see more than a third-class opera. Films seldom reached the villagers, and the sight of a newspaper in the country was an extreme rarity. There were, it is true, political cartoons about the evils of Christian missionaries from 1850 onwards, and in the anti-Japanese resistance days plenty of lively cartoons drawn on the sides of buildings. No one considered such things as art, though some were.

New ways in painting

The Chinese are natural cartoonists, finding it easy to extract the essence of a situation or a person's character and draw it simply and graphically. Much painting and sculpture nowadays tends to be basically a form of cartoon, in the sense that the essentials of the subject are extracted, exaggerated, personified and shown on heroic scale. The technique in both media is one previously unknown to Chinese art — heroic or socialist realism. Heroic and socialist may be fair adjectives, but the realism is really a form of idealization. The intention is realist but the result is idealist. None the less, the message gets across to the masses whose attention is continually attracted by the bright hopefulness of those posters, paintings and occasional sculptures.

Although pre-Renaissance art in the West often had the apparent impulsion to perfect its viewers, or to alter their outlook in one way or the other, post-Renaissance art has

A scene from the revolutionary ballet, The Red Detachment of Women. All forms of art in China are used to convey an ideological message — often this is brilliantly done. In this ballet the theme is the class struggle, and the strong story line tells the message both clearly and dramatically. The Chinese learned ballet from the Russians, and with their own traditional agility have added a dimension that is in some respects purely Chinese shown little of this attitude. The intent to perfect or improve people's attitudes and outlook on socialism is the salient feature of modern Chinese art.

Probably, in order to do what the Chinese Communists want to do — to bring about in the shortest possible time a thoroughly socialist state populated as nearly as possible by people who subscribe to socialist ideas—the present process is inevitable. The banishment, for the time being, of traditional forms of art in which some at least of the values of the old society were implicit or explicit has been completed. Doubtless in such a radical shift, in a sense not unlike the burning of the books that offended him by Shih-huang-ti so long ago, several babies have been thrown out with the bathwater. There are really no proper parallels. Never before in the history of man have 800 million people, blessed with the same language, been brought out of medievalism and national chaos in a couple of decades, to be given personal, job and family security. Obviously, from the Chinese point of view, the emphasis in art has to be on socialist communication and emulation, and the attempt has to be made to form an art that does this yet still remains popular. This inevitably leads to black and white impressions, even when the art is highly coloured. There are numerous hanging scrolls in traditional styles still painted, but in most of these the artist now inserts at a compositionally suitable place such symbols as a crowd of peasants with a sprinkling of red banners, striding among the mountains and mist. This approach, understandable as it is, seems less honest than that of the so-called socialist-realist school whose heroics are at least based on realism, whereas

A scene from a calendar of 1969. Mao is waving his cap to a group of young Red Guards. On his left is Lin Piao, still two years from his death in a plane crash as he fled to Russia after his plot against Mao was uncovered. On Mao's right is his wife, Chiang Ch'ing, and Chou En-lai in a pale blue suit

the mishmash of old and new approaches in one painting is fundamentally a contradiction. Back in 1959 I acquired in Peking a splendid scroll by an artist who paints camels and donkeys in the far north-west edge-of-the-desert areas. It shows a group of wonderfully proud camels led by an old Uighur peasant riding a donkey and playing a local guitar. On the central camel sits a Chinese girl who is carrying, quite inconspicuously, a bag with a tiny red cross on it. This is the local Communist cadre bringing medical help to the nomads and semi-nomads of the region as it was some thirteen or fourteen years ago. It is a very fine piece of spirited traditional painting, but I could do without the red cross.

Paintings and sculpture are bursting with rather naïve symbols, just as literature is bejewelled with loaded words and forced situations. In a novel by the modern writer Hao Jan, much thought of in China today, there are many passages such as the following. A peasant work-team leader's son has disappeared, and finally the truth dawns on the father.

"'A plot! The boy had been taken away by bad elements, or killed.... A plot—the last evil resort of the enemy in their hopeless struggle.'

"At this everything went black for a moment. But he [Hsiao Chang-chun] gritted his teeth and remained on his feet.... 'You're a Communist,' he told himself. 'Guns mustn't scare you, the threat of death shouldn't stop you. You should not give an inch in the face of the enemy's intrigues. We're making socialist revolution. In a revolution there's always sacrifice and bloodshed. You can't have a revolution without price. You've got to be able to stand this test!'"

And a little later:

"'Don't worry about me.... I can take this—and even a blow heavier than this. I live, I work and work hard not for myself, not for my son alone, but for all of us—for the revolution, for socialism. As long as we can keep our socialism safe it doesn't matter what I lose.'"

Hao Jan's books are very popular with China's reading public. For a Western reader, it is hard to believe in the character of Hsiao. He has been made into a cipher standing for steadfastness in the socialist cause. The rest, the agony of losing his son, feels as though it was added simply to heighten the message rather than for any other reason. But for the Chinese, with their innate sense of the fitting, the place that everything occupies in the scheme of things, of authority, of what is given—this opinion would not seem very valid. Socialism has already done a very great deal for them, and its defence is therefore acceptable....

The whole subject of the arts and communication is intimately bound up with a minority in the Chinese community known in Chinese as *chih-shih fen-tzu*—the "learned elements" or intellectuals. A difficult subject, and not least for the Communist Party in China.

To understand the problem in China it must be recalled that until the Revolution only a tiny minority of the population was literate, that a sizable number of these few could read only the simplest characters, and that this had always been so. If a Chinese official (a literate, dignified holder of the imperial patent, gained after passing the Imperial Examinations held almost yearly since Shih Huang-ti) wanted to go from his house to that of a colleague or friend with some written information which he had inscribed on a sheet of paper, that paper was not carried by the scholar, who never on any account was seen to

A painting of children playing at "Beating the Paper Tiger". Mao picked the old Chinese expression "paper tiger" to stigmatize the Americans during the Korean war. Characteristically the children are wielding such common objects as the rush-broom, a fly-swatter, a type of knife used in some provinces to reap the crops, and a traditional decorated sword

carry anything whatsoever, but by his servant. The idea that a literate man could possibly do any physical work such as rowing a boat on his favourite lake to see the sunrise mists among the spring willows, never entered that gentleman's head —or the head of anyone else, either. To be a scholar was to have, automatically, a position of respect. And, also automatically, to have only the remotest master-servant contact with the realities of life as it was known to the majority. The intellectuals of pre-Revolutionary China were more divorced by far from ordinary life than the intellectuals of any other country. To quote Mao Tse-tung's words from the *Yenan Forum*: they "seldom come into contact with the masses of workers, peasants and soldiers, and do not understand or study them, do not have intimate friends among them, and are not good at portraying them. When they do depict them, the clothes are the clothes of working people but the faces are those of petit-bourgeois intellectuals."

Their position now is all the more difficult for the intellectuals. To retain the respect to which they were accustomed, and to gain any sort of recognition in the present scheme of things, their outlook on people had to change radically. Many could not manage this drastic shift and have fallen into the limbo of unpublished artists. The intellectuals also had to alter their opinions on the arts themselves—away from the idea that art is for other *cognoscenti* towards the idea that art is for the people. This, too, proved an impossible step for most; and one can only sympathize with those who failed to make it and could not find a point of common ground with the exponents of the new aims of art in China. It is probably not possible for those who were artists of note in former times to do much more than bow out as gracefully as possible, making way, they can only hope, for young people whose life has been moulded by the new political system, and whose art expressions will naturally reflect that and not former systems. Again, it is worth quoting Mao: "Works of literature and art, as ideological forms, are products of the reflection in the human brain of the life of a given society. Revolutionary literature and art are the products of the reflection of the life of the people in the brains of revolutionary writers and artists."

What that art—those reflections —will be, we cannot at the moment tell: for none has really appeared. What have appeared are basically compromises between the techniques of the past and the messages of the present. The dead hand of

Russian painting was unfortunately laid rather early on the Chinese scene, and the blight of it is hard to cure. There are forms of painting in Western idioms, for example, that are nearer to being socialist in outlook and in aim than anything in Russia or China. There are new forms of theatre and of cinema, of literature, of journalism too, in the West that are closer to mass art forms than the rather primitive iconography of Chinese arts today.

If these are harsh words, they are sympathetically meant. Doubtless the inexorable needs of the continuing revolution and other matters in China require a quantity of emotive material in the written, histrionic and graphic fields, which should not in fact come under the heading "art" but under communication. The complaint that may justifiably be advanced is that in China nothing else is produced. Lu Hsun, that excellent writer of short stories from the twenties, so much admired today in China, managed to write in real terms about real people and at the same time show very clearly, because his people are so acutely observed and because his observation pierces to the roots of their situation in life, the political content of living. Much adulation of Lu Hsun in China has, alas, produced no real successor.

There is indeed a dilemma in the field of art in China. Perhaps the innate good sense of Chinese people, and their sense of humour (sadly lacking today in the arts) will solve the problem at some later date. In Russia the problem has not been solved, and the conflict between creative artists and the government continues as a sort of running battle —perhaps in some degree because the Soviet government is one that has long ceased to trust its own people. In China I would have higher hopes of a solution to the problem of new art in a new state for the reason that the Chinese have in the past produced vast quantities of art of true greatness, and because the Chinese government has shown in many ways, particularly the Cultural Revolution, that it is capable of trusting the Chinese people.

The illustration for the month of September on a 1969 calendar. The portrait of Mao is flanked by two banners in the sky, reading (left), "Long Live the Chinese Communist Party", and (right), "Long Live Mao". The other slogans deal with the central and key role of the Communist Party in life (on the left) and (right) the importance of Marxist ideology in all thinking, while the central slogan lauds the Revolutionary Committee. The two large characters, one at either side, held up by people joyously waving the Little Red Book, are the traditional ones meaning Double Happiness

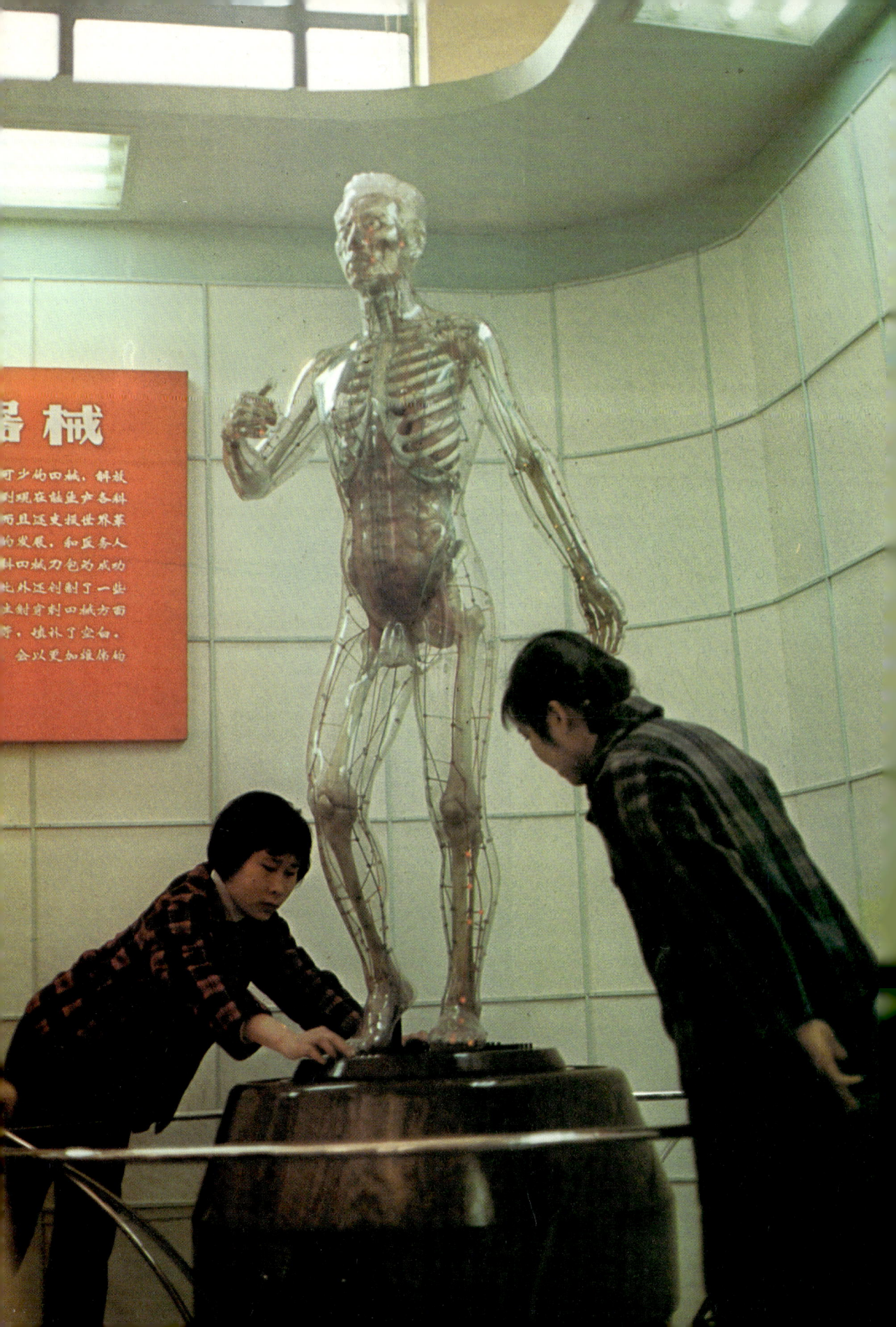

CHAPTER FIVE

SCIENCE AND ITS APPLICATION

Twenty years ago the words "Chinese science" pronounced in intelligent circles West or East, would have produced a look of puzzlement, or at least polite scepticism. Three hundred and fifty years ago, the same words heard in the same circles in Europe would have met with ready recognition among those who knew anything of China, for at that time European achievements in science and technology were less advanced than those of the Chinese. Today, thanks to one of the most remarkable works of scientific scholarship of this century, the multi-volume *Science and Civilisation in China* by Joseph Needham, there is no excuse for ignorance about Chinese achievements in basic sciences and in many aspects of technology, which often antedated their counterparts in the West by several centuries.

But we are concerned with China today. Here, too, there is an astonishing story of development in the past two decades. Apart altogether from the surprisingly rapid success in nuclear fission and the manufacture of guided missiles requiring technology of an extremely high order, other less controversial avenues have been explored in Chinese scientific work. What may prove to be one of the most important advances in medicine since the introduction of general anaesthesia—a method of supplanting it in certain cases by the use of acupuncture—has surprised and fascinated the world at large. Less dramatic but even more far-reaching in its implications for hundreds of millions of people is the progress made in taming the turbulent rivers of China—a process involving some of the oldest Chinese scientific skills such as irrigation, hydraulics and the use of a massive labour force, together with some of the newer ones such as heavy industrial manufacture. Yet another field of activity is archaeology, a scientific discipline introduced into China only a matter of fifty years ago. In the last two decades, work on discovering and preserving the Chinese past has expanded excitingly, producing a galaxy of results that have begun to share the spotlight with acupuncture. The publication in 1971 and 1972 of tomb discoveries rivalling in interest and importance those of Tutankhamun fifty years ago, has served to focus world attention not only on the discoveries but also on a China turning to more out-going international policies, and perhaps to a period of consolidation after the lessons of the recent past at home.

Acupuncture

The Chinese press is full of stories about medical work, its successes,

A life-size figure showing the acupuncture points. Their position on the surface and in relation to the skeleton can be clearly seen. On the stand is a series of buttons so arranged that, to find out which acupuncture points relate to which variety of treatment, and which are related to each other in various ways, on depression the relevant points light up. Acupuncture has been brought into focus by its intensive use in China lately, and the significance of the traditional points has been confirmed by a Russian named Kirlian, who has perfected an apparatus that generates a high-frequency electrical field, and has an optical viewer. When parts of the body are placed in the field, the strong points of light seen bear no relation to any anatomical structure, but tally with the traditional acupuncture points

One of the treacherous gorges of the Middle Yangtze River. Since 1949, much has been done to tame the Yangtze by damming at various places, especially upstream, and thus controlling the volume of water at different seasons. Some of the worst hazards of the gorges have been removed by blasting, and navigational beacons have been installed. The river is navigable all year round for ocean-going ships up to Wuhan, and smaller vessels can reach Ipin in Szechuan province

its targets, its problems. This is not surprising in a country where doctors were formerly rare and largely for the rich, where first-aid was unknown except perhaps in large towns, where before the Revolution it is doubtful if there were hospital beds for more than a few thousand of the 650 million population.

A recent small report is fairly typical. It describes how an army medical team headed by a woman doctor began working in the Canton school for deaf mutes in December 1968. Starting at once to treat what seemed to be the most suitable but intractable cases by acupuncture, they now claim what they modestly call "some success" with 80 per cent of their patients. Describing a typical good result they cite the case of a fifteen-year-old boy who had been deaf from birth and was unable to produce any intelligible sound, pre-sumably not having had specialized speech therapy. He is now able to hear and can sing songs. It is of course unlikely that a deaf mute of this age will catch up mentally with his own age group, but the remarkable success of simple acupuncture treatment in such cases is underlined in a human way. Further detailed clinical reports over a period of time will be needed before the claims can be accepted and the treatment established as a prime therapeutic measure.

The most dramatic use of acupuncture, apart from this cure for certain forms of deafness, and also the cure of certain cases of blindness, is its use as an anaesthetic to replace inhalation or intravenous general anaesthesia in major and minor surgery. News of this reached the Western world only comparatively recently, but in fact the technique was pioneered in Shanghai and was first used there in 1958. About that time there was great activity in Peking in the Institute for Chinese Medicine where experiments were being undertaken on Western lines to determine what happens when acupuncture needles are inserted in the traditional places for the relief, improvement or cure of disease. I remember watching several experiments, making extensive notes on them and later discussing with the medical personnel the results that seemed to indicate that there are lines of communication within the tissues of the human body not defined by any Western anatomical or physiological research or knowledge. Experiments at that time seemed to show that certain of the tissue planes have a greater capacity to conduct galvanic electricity than other parts of the tissues. No one, however, suggested a full explanation had been arrived at.

It was interesting at that time, too, to attend classes where the "model" into which the acupuncture needles were inserted was a life-size Sung bronze, made for teaching purposes in those far-off days. This bronze figure had several hundred small holes drilled in it, each corresponding to the correct point at which a needle may be inserted in the human body. In former times, the surface of the bronze was covered by a layer of opaque wax, and the hollow interior was filled with water. When the student inserted his needle he was rewarded when he hit the right spot by a thin stream of water, quickly staunched by pinching the wax together again.

The procedure called acupuncture (derived from Latin *acus*, "needle" and *pungere*, "to sting") is called in Chinese *chen-chiu*, literally "needle (and) heat". This refers to the needle treatment in combina-

Army men working on an archaeological site

One of two burial suits of jade pieces wired together with gold. Jade pieces with corner holes have long been known to collectors, but not until recent excavation was their origin and purpose revealed

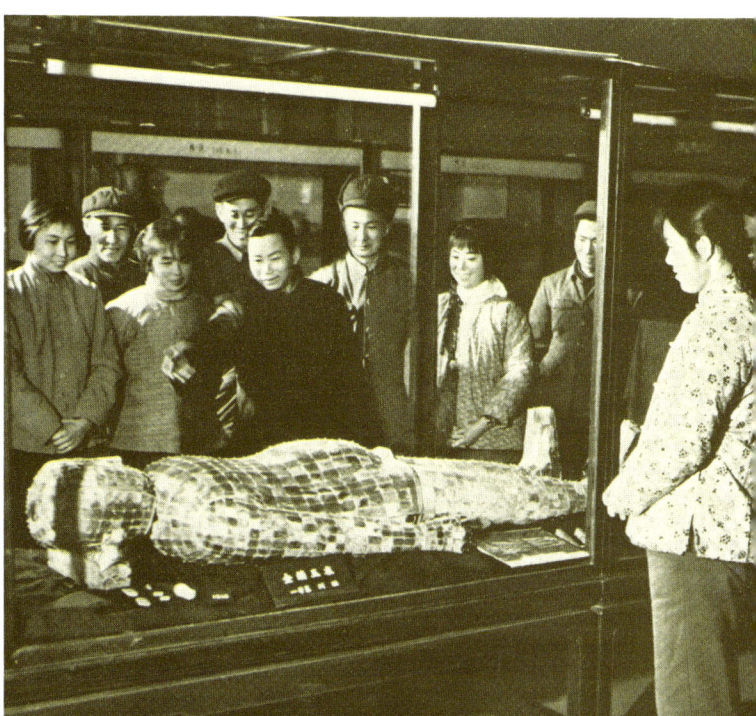

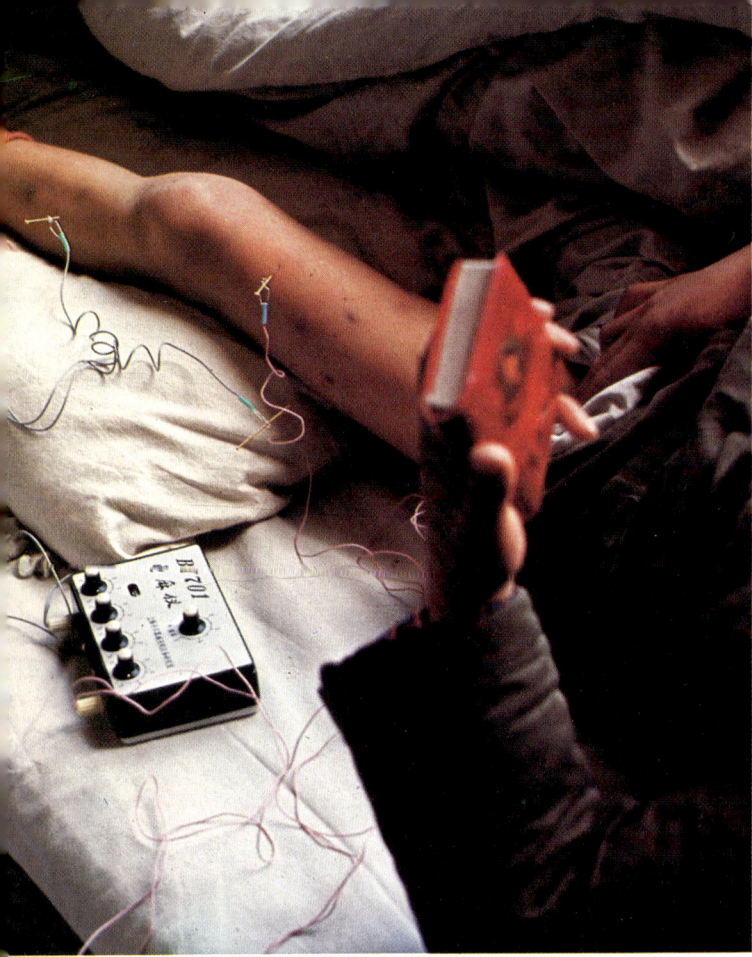

A patient with two acupuncture needles inserted into his leg In this case a galvanic electrical stimulus is being used

Opposite: a young girl with acupuncture needles on which herbal packets are smouldering—a treatment named moxibustion

An ancient bronze life-size cast used in teaching acupuncture

tion with what is called moxibustion —the burning of a herb called mugwort (*Artemisia vulgaris*) near the points of needle insertion, and sometimes even attached to the handles of the needles themselves. These processes, together with the use of herbs from the extremely extensive Chinese pharmacopoeia, and certain physiotherapeutic measures such as massage and controlled breathing exercises, constitute the main body of Chinese traditional medicine. Chinese physicians claim to be able to distinguish over seventy different types of pulse.

The traditional Chinese explanation of how acupuncture works is based on the idea that there is a flow of vital energy (*ch'i*) through the body—a flow that is under the general control of the *yin* and the *yang*. When the *yin-yang* balance is incorrect, disease results due to interruption, irregularity, or other abnormality in the flow of vital energy. The whole body is divided into *yin* organs (spleen, liver and heart being three) and *yang* organs (stomach, large intestine and others). The vital energy flows along mysterious *ching-lo*, paths of communication beneath the surface of the body. There are twelve of these paths, or meridians, on either side of the body (representing the organs), another running along the vertical midline of the body in front, and yet another at the back. The insertion points for acupuncture needles lie on these lines. The exact places at which needles are inserted to obtain various curative effects in different diseases is highly complex, the balancing of *yin* and *yang* organs being involved.

As far back as the early 1960s, interest in the subject made me spend quite a lot of time watching acupuncture treatment of polio victims, mostly small children, in the

Institute for Chinese Medicine in Peking where some apparently worthwhile results were being obtained in stimulating the damaged faculties of the nerves that carry the impulses that make muscles move. Many migraine patients assured me that they had experienced great

arthritis in his hands, which had screwed the joints up and prevented him from having much use of his fingers. He had come to Peking as a last resort, and after acupuncture treatment over several months was able to assist a friend to draw fine maps. We do not know enough as

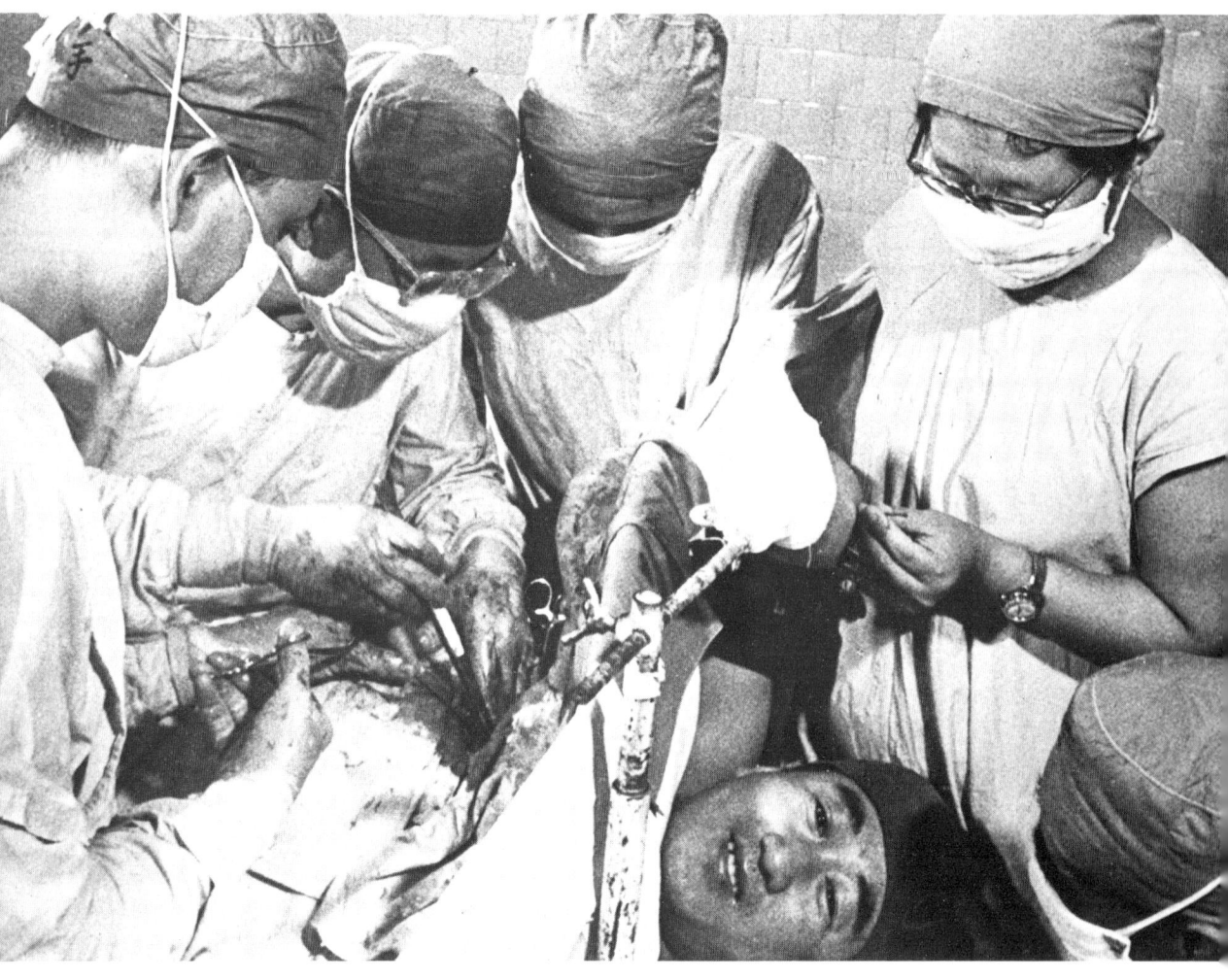

Acupuncture anaesthesia. A single needle continuously vibrated by the man on the right produced perfect anaesthesia for this lung operation. The patient's smile tells its own story

relief, not so much from the headaches themselves, but because the attacks were much less frequent.

Various forms of arthritis seemed to respond to acupuncture, too. Staying in the Hsin Chiao (New Overseas Chinese) Hotel in Peking at that time was an Australian doctor in his thirties who had been severely afflicted with a form of

yet to judge what the place of acupuncture in medical treatment will eventually be, but that it will have a value is fairly sure.

When the first Chinese accounts of acupuncture anaesthesia in major chest and abdominal surgery were published in the Chinese press, Western medical men were not unnaturally sceptical. The implication of those gory operating-theatre photographs, the smiling face of the patient separated only by a barrier of cloth from the sight of his own entrails, the anaesthetist busily twirling a needle or two in the forearm, seemed too good to be true. The beginning of Western belief in the truth of the matter came when a film taken of such an operation was shown on television, the patient calmly getting down from the operating table after having been sewn up. Finally, several teams of Western doctors visited China and observed the whole process from start to finish. They were actually instructed in acupuncture methods by the Chinese, and came back to try it out for themselves.

It has been known in China for a long time that inserting needles at points such as one between the thumb and forefinger relieves pain in cases of toothache and stomach cramp. The Chinese argued from this during the 1950s that the anaesthetic effect so achieved could be used to obviate pain before it was produced by surgery. And so it proved to be. Now it is commonplace in China, patients being given the choice between conventional anaesthesia and acupuncture. The advantages of the latter are several: there is no danger to the cardiac system and no depression in breathing rate, no chance of kidney or liver damage from the chemicals of ordinary anaesthetic agents, and there are no side-effects or after-effects. Even delivery of babies by Caesarean operations is done under acupuncture. It is traditionally said that there is an acupuncture point that aborts a pregnancy, but no reports of such a procedure being attempted, in a country where abortion is legal, have been heard.

The somewhat metaphysical Chinese theory of how acupuncture works has several Western rivals, most of them also matters of conjecture, involving supposed interference with the physical structures that carry messages of pain to the brain. But, so far, it has to be admitted that the way in which acupuncture really works, either as

an anaesthetic or as a therapeutic agent, is unknown. The fact that it does, however, is now undisputed and its use as an anaesthetic may well come to constitute one of this century's most important medical advances.

Water surging through an aperture in one of China's huge new dams. Apart from flood control, most large dams produce huge quantities of cheap electricity

Old and new methods

The whole field of medicine in

A canal constructed by commune peasants to lead water to areas where it is needed. Thousands of square miles of formerly waste land have been irrigated by such small but important local undertakings. In the winter season most communes continue to extend and improve their irrigation and other facilities. It is not uncommon for the peasants to straighten the course of a local river in order to rationalize the location and use of available land

China is one of great activity. The shortage of doctors for 800 million people is the spur that urges on not only the making of discoveries and experimenting with new techniques, but full use by the Chinese of their traditional medical men. Unlike Western countries, which threw their traditional medical lore out of the window opened by the advance of modern scientific techniques, the Chinese are being much more prudent. The expansion and consolidation of old remedial treatments of all kinds and the systematic training of young men and women in the old style of medicine were begun very soon after 1949. Research on a large scale on Western lines was also begun at that time into the whole field of herbal medicine. And sure enough it was soon found that many a herb used from time immemorial contained agents recognized by modern medicine to be of value against the diseases for which such herbs had always been used.

The arts of surgery too have progressed, and the Chinese seem able to regraft limbs severed in accidents with remarkable success. The accent in Chinese medicine today is on the necessary, the humane, and the possible. The so-called "bare-foot doctors"—simply people who have undergone some first-aid and simple medical training enabling them to deal with common complaints, common accidents that occur in the fields—need not have caused the derision they did in the Western press. Many of the diagnoses and treatments of everyday medical practice can easily be made and given by people with minimal requirement of sophisticated equipment. Faced with the magnitude of the problem of bringing medical care to all as rapidly as possible, the Chinese have chosen various handy expedients and stop-gap procedures, as well as forging ahead with the expansion of more conventional Chinese and Western medical education. In China today there is a refreshing absence of that aura of professional mystique pervading many a Western medical institution—a refreshing absence of the feeling elsewhere in the world that medical people belong to an in-group, and that patients are incapable of understanding medicine.

Taming the rivers

Medicine, in the West at least, is a glamorous subject. Irrigation, water conservancy, fertilizers, ploughing methods, planting techniques, geological prospecting, climatology, education, oil technology and similar subjects do not make many headlines. Yet in China, backward China as most Chinese will tell you, they do. The Chinese are nothing if not a practical and reasonable people. This is one's general experience of them. And with the new rationality that has entered into their lives in most aspects they are also fast becoming remarkable as innovators.

The old myth of the Great Yü who tirelessly worked until he had tamed the rampaging Yellow River, has now been made almost completely fact. Millions of Great Yüs have finally got very near to completing the projects which have already firmly placed in history the disastrous flooding of the Yellow River. The river is over 3,000 miles (4,800 kilometres) long and its basin covers nearly half a million square miles (over one million square kilometres). There are 50 million acres (20 million hectares) and 110 million people in the valleys of the upper and middle reaches and on the plains of the lower parts of the river. In the 2,000 years before the Revolution there were more than 1,500 major floods from the lower section of the river, and 26 major changes in its course. If you had taken a boat down the Yellow River prior to 1853, or again between 1938 and 1947, you would have arrived not at the Gulf of Chihli, north of the Shantung Peninsula, but, with a certain semantic felicity, at the Yellow Sea to the south of the peninsula. A glance at a map will confirm the profound nature of this variation in the river's course. In and around that fan-shaped area millions, probably scores of millions, of people have perished from drowning and starvation and disease in the years of flood.

The problem was silt. The river's upper and middle reaches run through the world's largest loess highland area. When rain fell there in former days, the loose topsoil of the hills, bearing little vegetation, was easily eroded, and each year about 1,600 million tons were carried downstream to the lower reaches. This volume of silt—1,452 million cubic yards (1,110 million cubic metres) of it—was deposited on the river-bed as the rate of water-flow progressively slackened, raising the bed and encouraging massive floods. Dikes built by the peasants over a period of more than two thousand years had to be raised each year in the hope that they would be high enough to contain the water. In many places, for long stretches, the bed of the river was many feet higher than the surrounding land.

The problem was tackled in several ways. Slowly, by hand, every yard of erodable soil in the drainage area was terraced, or stabilized either by cover crops or by the planting of hundreds of millions of trees. Hundreds of thousands of tiny and not so tiny dams were built in gulleys and on every tributary, so that less silt was washed away, and much of that was caught by the larger dams. The water reaching the river's main course carried an ever-decreasing load of silt. The huge San Men Dam was

An excavated, animal-shaped pot dating to Neolithic times. Other, more remarkable, examples have come to light in the last fifteen years in scientifically controlled excavation in such areas as Shantung, Kansu and Honan provinces. They date from the 3rd and 2nd millennia B.C.

Top: a ritual bronze basin, p'an, with a pattern that originated as a monster-mask, t'ao-t'ieh, but preserves little but the eye. The piece is dated in the Shang period around the 16th–15th centuries B.C.

Above: bronze ho, or ritual wine-pourer, in the shape of a round box with bird lid, tiger handle and monster spout. Western Chou, 9th century B.C.

and many smaller lakes are stocked with fish. And that soupy, ochre water that used to pour with vicious strength through the San Men Gorge, is fast losing its yellow colour.

The stunning successes of the Yellow River projects are duplicated on an even larger scale on the Yangtze, and there are other great schemes in varying stages of completion on the Huai and the Haiho rivers. The major potential of these four rivers has already been harnessed, and their powers of destruction largely eliminated. The old saying, "three summers, one harvest", common in those regions, is no longer true.

Finding ancient treasures

From flood control to archaeology may seem a long step, but it was precisely in connection with the control of the Yellow River that a massive archaeological effort in China got under way. Since then, many another discovery has been the result of decisions to remodel part of the landscape to assist in irrigation or to utilize land more economically.

In the early fifties work began on preparing the site at San Men Sha on the middle Yellow River for the building of the huge dam and hydro-electric generating station. The site itself, a deep rocky gorge with three channels formed by two islands in the stream, was one much celebrated in myth and local folklore. At San Men (Three Gates), boats had to be navigated with caution downstream through the race of the water. The upstream passage could only be made by teams of trackers straining on ropes to pull the boats by main force against the current, treading narrow catwalks cut hundreds of years ago in the cliffs. The names of the "gates"—Gate of the

built, forming a great lake behind it that will eventually stretch back about 100 miles (160 kilometres). Its hydro-electric station generates very considerable quantities of power (well over one million kilowatts) to run a new town, to energize pumps for irrigation and drainage of farmlands long dry or waterlogged. Part of the old course of the Yellow River in Honan province has been converted into a canal which has now irrigated an area of 100,000 acres (40,500 hectares). The danger of flooding is now largely averted, the total area of useful land has increased, vast forests of new trees are growing (with beneficial effects on climate), new millions of kilowatts of electricity are generated, one huge

Gods, Gate of Ghosts, Gate of Man —tell their own story about the degrees of navigability of the river in the gorge.

By 1957 the ancient rock-cut inscriptions on the walls of the gorge had been either removed or copied, and the Academia Sinica in Peking had been spurred on to make a survey of the whole area to be affected either by rising water behind the dam, by ancillary installations, or by the building of a new city some distance from the southern bank of the river. The importance of the region, almost in the centre of the ancient lands of Shang and Chou civilization, made time a crucial factor, and all methods including those of the tomb-robbers of old were pressed into service. A common sight in those years was that of a hundred or more local men each thrusting a long wooden pole vertically into the soft loess ground. On the end of each pole was a metal cylinder which brought up to the surface a vertical section, some three inches (76 millimetres) or so in depth, of the ground at the lower level. The peasant archaeological workers soon learned to identify a stratum, or "floor", of different colour or texture, and the foremen (also peasants) noted down the depth and position—there was a man with a pole every 6 feet (2 metres), in a regular pattern. Thus, with unskilled labour, very large areas below ground could be mapped with fair accuracy in minimal time, their approximate content assessed, and its depth ascertained. In this way, magnificent work was begun on important Neolithic sites yielding quantities of splendid *yangshao* and *lungshan* pottery and other remains, and confirming the various forms taken by the habitations of those days. Another result was the discovery of the supremely interesting burials of Shang and Chou nobility, containing a treasure-trove of gold and bronze and, equally important, permitting a clearer picture to be formed of precisely dateable times in these periods.

Perhaps the most interesting and significant of the discoveries of those years at San Men was the burial-ground of the Guo nobility at San Tsuen Ling. Dating for this is completely certain since the Eastern Chou times date from 770 B.C. and the capital of the Guo state, Shang Yang, was captured by a neighbouring state in 665 B.C. So the tombs all date to those hundred and five years. More than fifty tombs were found in the immediate area, one of them

Two leopards of parcel-gilt bronze inlaid with silver and garnets. The superb workmanship of these two figures is unmatched in any other Han dynasty objects known. They were discovered in 1968 in the tomb of the princess Tou Wan at Man-ch'eng in Hopei province. The more usual jade carvings of pigs which were used in tombs to weight the edges and corners of the funeral dress and other cloth coverings, were replaced in the princess's tomb by these exquisite pieces. There were two pairs in the tomb.
The excavation was remarkable in that it revealed a large number of objects whose conception and workmanship show a whole range of Han dynasty skills in a series of extremely beautiful things made of bronze, jade and pottery

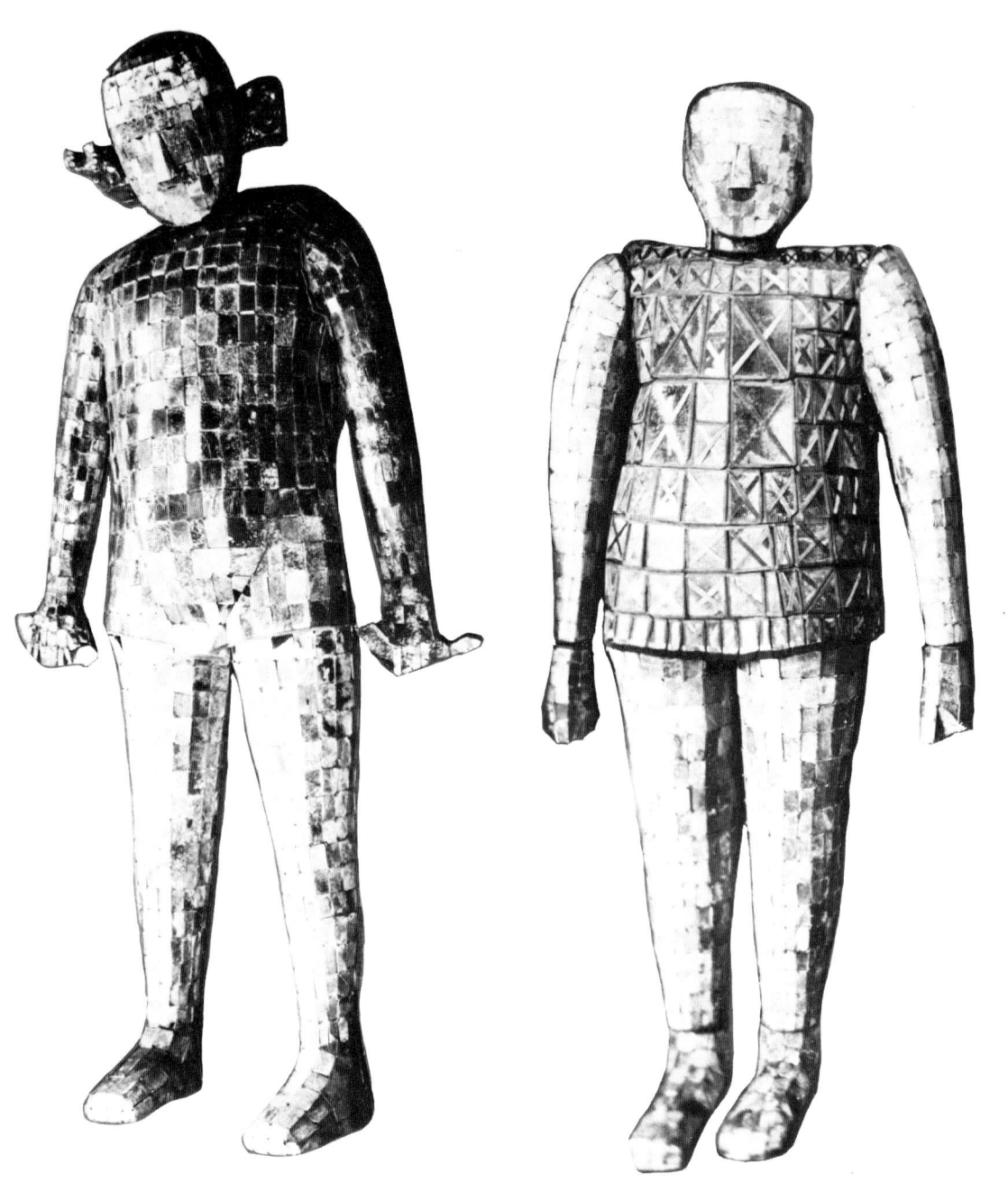

The jade suits of Prince Liu Sheng and his wife Tou Wan, dating from the late 2nd century B.C. Each suit is composed of over 2,000 pieces of jade laced together with gold wire. The suits are not of great beauty, but of unique interest

belonging to a ruler of Guo, Yuen Tuo. To him, most probably, belonged the twenty chariots of lacquered wood, fitted with bronze bells and hub-caps, each pulled by two horses. On the death of the ruler, the whole score of vehicles had been driven into a specially prepared long pit which was then filled in. A remarkable piece of fine excavation was carried out, revealing the complete line of chariots with their horses in skeletal form, the bronze parts and bells still in the relative positions.

There was a feeling of the closeness of the past, the very Chinese past, in this yellow land. In another burial-pit, a dog had run in with the horses, and its skeleton was found beneath the floor of the chariot, adding yet one more little facet of human ordinariness to the ancient scene. Apart from the gorge itself, no rock is to be seen in the whole landscape for fifty or more miles around. The hills mount in giant steps as if some omnipotent and playful geographer had ordered mankind to follow his contour lines in three-dimensional loess. To the horizon in all directions the hills rise in geometrically conceived shapes and there is scarcely a yard that is not contrived by man. Somehow it is not surprising to find the history of China from the Neolithic onward in this compact and preservative earth.

More spectacular than these discoveries, even more interesting than the opening in the late 1950s of the late Ming emperor Wan-li's tomb outside Peking, were the announcements in 1971 and 1972 of the discovery of much richer tombs. The first was found near Mancheng in Hopei province, not very far from Peking, when People's Liberation Army men, working on a hillside, uncovered pieces of dressed stone and made a report to the archaeological section of the Academia Sinica. This occurred in 1968 as the Western press were assuring the world at large that the Red Guards had put paid to all that was old in China! The site proved to contain two tombs of the Western Han dynasty (206 B.C.–A.D. 23), the occupant of one being Prince Liu Sheng, elder brother of the emperor Wu; and of the other, his wife Tou Wan. The bodies of both had been enclosed in cases shaped more or less like their human contents, each consisting of more than two thousand pieces of jade, pierced at the corners and sewn together with pounds and pounds of gold wire. Ironically, these precious suits, designed to ward off all dangers and evils, contained only the dust into which the royal couple had long since turned. In the two underground chambers, each about 3,900 cubic yards (3,000 cubic metres) in volume, were about 2,800 objects—vessels of bronze, silver, gold and jade, together with pottery, lacquer-ware, silk fabrics, chariots and the harnesses of their horses. The entry to the tombs had been cunningly sealed by molten iron poured into the cavity of a hollow wall.

A far cry, these splendid tombs, from others found in Shantung and Shansi provinces about the same time, containing the remains of slaves who were human sacrifices at Shang and Chou dynasty noble burials.

The Marquis's Lady

In the following year, 1972, an even more fascinating newly discovered tomb was announced. Dating to the same Western Han dynasty as did the tombs of Prince Liu Sheng and his wife, this sepulchre contained the almost life-like body of the wife of the Marquis of Ta, a minor aristocrat. The site is on the outskirts of the ancient city of Changsha whose history goes back three thousand years. As early as the Chou dynasty, Changsha was known for its metal-work, its textiles and its lacquer-ware. During Western Han

The outer of three lacquered coffins within which lay the remarkably preserved body of the wife of the Marquis of Ta, a minor aristocrat who lived between 193 and 141 B.C. It is seen in situ as the excavation was in progress, and the inner wooden walls of the tomb stand round it. The excavation and the extremely detailed examination of everything discovered, forms the subject of one of the most fascinating of all documentary films. The film follows the process of finding and dismantling the tomb, the examination of all its varied contents, with an intelligent and detailed commentary on every aspect

times it was the seat of the local ruler, and its economy was highly sophisticated. The tomb was discovered in a chamber about 52 feet (16 metres) under the summit of a mound in the rolling country there, the mound being made principally of rammed earth brought from other parts of the country. The burial chamber itself was surrounded on all sides by an ingenious jacket composed of a layer of charcoal between 12 and 16 inches (30 and 40 centimetres) thick, itself sealed on the inner and outer sides by a layer of white sticky clay.

Inside this elaborate protective envelope lay the tomb, a box-like chamber made of three layers of wooden planking, sitting on three large logs at the base of the pit. The box contained three wooden sarcophagi, one inside the other, surrounded by the multifarious possessions buried with the dead woman. The three coffins fit one within the other with almost no intervening space. The outer one is lacquered in black with lively cloud-like shapes in yellow and white seeming to float on the surfaces, animal and other forms playing between them. All the joints of the coffins are carefully made mortise and tenon work. The vermilion-lacquered middle coffin is decorated on its lid with clouds and a design of two dragons and two tigers fighting. Its sides have geometric-pattern borders enclosing magnificent designs of mountains and clouds among which frolic dragons, deer and monsters. The entire design of this middle coffin is more forceful and striking than that of the cool and dreamy outer one.

A remarkable T-shaped piece of painted silk was found draping the inner coffin, the first complete painting on silk from this time, 2,100 years ago. The upper third has a large vermilion sun against which a bird stands in silhouette, and below it a *fusang* (mulberry) tree between whose branches appear eight smaller suns—possibly referring to the old myth about Yi the Archer who shot down nine suns. The upper left area has a thin crescent moon with a toad and a rabbit, and just below that is a scene from the old myth about Lady Chang Ngo flying to the moon.

The middle section of the silk is occupied by a charming scene in which an old woman (probably the person buried within) leaning on her stick and escorted by three attendants seems to be talking to two kneeling male figures. This small segment in itself is a considerable work of art, beautifully balanced in forms and in the distribution of the colours. Below, amid the swirling, snake-like bodies of heraldic dragons, is a feast, while at the bottom are emblems of sea and land.

The innermost coffin is covered with silk decorated with patterns made of coloured feathers enclosed in a border of satin-stitch. The occupant of the coffin was a woman of about fifty, rather stout, and miraculously preserved. She was wrapped in over twenty layers of silk and linen, lying on her back, the head towards the north. There was almost no sign of deterioration, the skin coloration being almost normal, the connective tissue beneath it (according to the doctors of Hunan Medical College) still soft. The colour of the femoral arteries or main arteries of the legs, was about the same as it would be in a newly dead person.

There is a film of this discovery in which one of the astonishing sights is a close-up of a doctor's finger being pressed into the upper arm of the woman, which dents and flattens out again almost as it would on a live person. Without doubt the wife of the Marquis of Ta is the best-preserved corpse of this era ever to be found. It is thought that the charcoal and clay envelope together with the conditions of soil structure and humidity are responsible for the nearly perfect condition of the tomb's contents.

Were the coffins, the silk drape and the person of the Marquis's lady all that the tomb contained, it would still be an important discovery. But its contents were many, presenting a picture of the life and times of a great lady of two thousand years ago—enough to stock what will perhaps be one of the

The funeral banner of painted silk found draped over the inner coffin. Apart from 50 pieces of clothing including stockings, shoes and gloves, there were 70 pieces of silk fabric in the tomb, mostly well preserved. The banner is 81 inches (205 centimetres) long and the width of the upper part is 36 inches (92 centimetres). It is painted with a large number of ritual, legendary, mythological and other subjects, including a group of figures about the middle, one of whom may well represent the woman interred

The condition of the body tissues of the woman was extremely supple. In the documentary film the autopsy is preceded by X-ray photography and various injection techniques that revealed gallstones. The woman probably died of coronary thrombosis —a heart attack

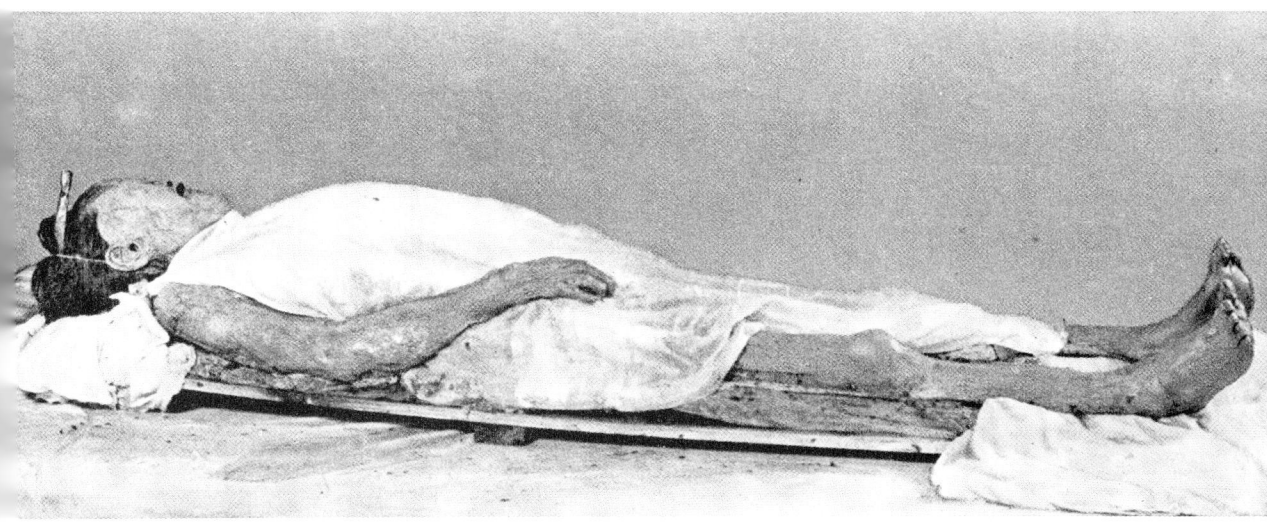

Four of the 162 wooden tomb figurines buried with the Marquis of Ta's wife. Some of the figures were dressed in real clothes, while on others, such as these, the clothes were carved and painted. The two standing figures are playing an instrument made of bamboo tubes connected at the base to a gourd and stopped like a flute. This is still in use in China and is called a shêng. The kneeling figures play the Chinese zither, se. These formed part of a banquet scene

richest and most fascinating little museums in the world, if the Chinese decide to keep all the material together in one place.

Some idea of the sophistication of the contents emerges from examining one silk-gauze gown with long wide sleeves, which is as light as if it were made of the finest nylon net of today. There were silken stockings, shoes and gloves, and more than seventy other pieces of silk—plain, rich brocades and damasks in browns of several shades, silks with patterns of pale yellow, grey, dark red, vermilion, blue-greens and white. Designs of superb quality and inventiveness were painted, sometimes with gold and silver, on many of the silks.

Nearly two hundred pieces of the finest lacquerware in perfect condition were in the tomb. They include containers of many types, varying from exquisitely fitted toilet-boxes to eating-bowls and, perhaps the most beautiful of all, oval cups with ears. Many pieces are inscribed with the owner's name or with "for the use of the lord", and some have fine incised lines on them no broader than a hair. Pottery in the tomb mostly contained foodstuffs—fruit such as melon and peach, dried ginger, aromatic herbs, bean curd and, of course, rice and wheat products. There were also chicken bones, fish and lotus root in the lacquer dishes. The same ingredients would be entirely normal in a Chinese kitchen today.

Three rarities in tomb furnishings were also found. A wooden zither, found in a brocade bag, was in excellent condition, its twenty-five strings and their frets undamaged. The second musical instrument was a *yu*, a set of bamboo pipes blown through a single tube and stopped like a flute. With it was a set of twelve pitch pipes with the pitch of each marked on the bottom in black ink. All of these instruments can be played today, and modern versions are still part of a Chinese orchestra's equipment.

Another interesting find was a set of 312 bamboo slips inscribed with characters on the inner, yellow, side —the other being still deep green as it was when split two thousand years ago. The slips were strung at top and bottom with fine hempen cords (see page 9 for how the character for "book" came about) and the characters, in square script, give a detailed account of the contents of the tomb, which is apparently almost accurate. With these were forty-eight bamboo baskets whose contents range from clothing, bolts of silk and straw hats, to foodstuffs and several hundred pieces of un-baked clay money.

"Most notable," as a Chinese account says, is the set of 162 wooden figurines representing entertainers at a banquet. Eighteen figurines were dressed in real clothes and another eight have painted vestments. Three attendants are standing and the remainder are the members of a song and dance group. In one little group of five, three are playing miniature zithers, while two more in their midst have the *yu* pipes to their mouths.

The picture of aristocratic life revealed as you consider the rich sophistication of the buried material is a luxurious one. The Marquis of Ta was merely one of numerous minor feudal lords, deriving his revenues from about 700 families only. And from this comparatively small number of working persons he was able to furnish his wife's tomb—apart at all from his own palace and daily living needs—in amazing luxury.

The Chinese have two attitudes to the story of the tomb. One is that the skill of the Chinese craftsmen who contrived these deeply satisfying objects has hardly been surpassed anywhere in the world. And the second attitude is to underline the large-scale exploitation of the people spelled out all too clearly in the quality and cost of the objects in terms of work and money. We can hardly disagree with either attitude. But perhaps as a means of teaching the horrors of the class structure, it is not the most forceful. For in the end what one remembers is the ravishing beauty of the silks, of the lacquer, and the reality of the mythology which evidently inspired the makers of the painted silk and painted coffins with their playful yet dreamlike fantasies.

Thinking more carefully of the actual craftsmen who made such marvellous and beautiful things, it is obvious that they must have been in some way a privileged group—no one who is starving, who is miserable and has no hope in life, could invent such gay and imaginative designs or sustain that inventive process in the same vein throughout large works. As to the ordinary subjects of the Marquis of Ta, we can only conjecture—but most of them must have been near to slavery.

More than 180 pieces of fine lacquerware were in the tomb, most having retained their original clear colours. The five large bowls, one oval eared cup and two mugs with handles sit on the tray where they were placed over two thousand years ago. The designs in black on vermilion include stylized leaves, petals, clouds and animals. The design and conception of these vessels reveal the richness and the subtlety of the Han craftsman's mind, as do the magnificent, opulent and often mysterious patterns on the three coffins themselves

117

CHAPTER SIX

THE FUTURE

It is a welcome and also a very remarkable thought, if we recall the chaos of China only a quarter of a century ago, to be able to predict a future other than deeper chaos and total anarchy. But this is precisely what can be done with considerable confidence now, for perhaps the first time in over a hundred years.

By the end of 1972, China was beginning to emerge from a period of self-imposed isolation which was her reaction to the internal problems she had to begin solving, and also to the general hostility of the rest of the world. This Chinese reaction, the turn inward, followed eventually by more out-going policies, is a pattern often seen in the past when a new régime took over in China, the commencement of the Ming dynasty being an excellent and in some ways quite similar example. For at that time, as at the Revolution of 1949, China had just managed to regain control of its own affairs from foreigners.

China has now joined the United Nations Organization on her own terms, as she always said she intended to do, and has received visits from an American president repudiating much of America's stance *vis-à-vis* China in the past quarter of a century, and from the Prime Minister of Japan, the former despoiler of China, in apparently accommodating mood. Meanwhile Russia is hastening to make overtures to a united Europe in an effort to secure her western flank and permit her to concentrate on her eastern borders with China.

The Chinese attitude to Russia is one of disapproval of Russian ideology, and massive defensive preparation in case of Russian military adventures directed against her. Whether open war between Russia and China will come, is a question no one can answer except the Russians. The chances are that it will be avoided if only because China, showing few signs of warlike attitudes towards any state, will tend to have more natural allies and supporters than Russia—always provided that America does not repudiate its dove-like words on the subject of peace with China. It seems probable that India and China will compose their differences in the not-too-distant future.

As to the internal future of China, there are things that can be said with complete certainty, and others that must remain in the realm of probability.

Certain it is that China will remain a land of basically agricultural wealth for many years to come. Its former extremely backward agriculture has already been transformed into a type of farming that is more rational and therefore infinitely more efficient. But in order to take the

The lush plain of Mangshih in southwest Yunnan near the border with Burma. This is a tropical area and fine rice-crops are reaped from the fields by the Tai people who are the predominant inhabitants. They are related to the Thai in Thailand—a people who slowly migrated from China via Yunnan and the several large rivers that run southward through the province. The fields in the foreground have been newly planted with rice seedlings. The numerous thatched huts here and there are watch-huts from which birds and other predators can be scared off. Fruit, bamboos, all manner of tropical vegetation including the lac tree (Rhus vernicifera), from whose sap lacquer is made, grow here. The hills are thinly populated by peoples at a much lower level of cultural development, of whom the Ch'ing-po, who are pantheists, are one

Chairman Mao greets prime minister Kakuei Tanaka of Japan in the study of his small apartment in Peking. The Chairman lives extremely simply, and seems to spend most of his waking time in this book-lined room. The gradual thawing of relations between China and Japan must be seen at least partly in the light of what China considers the greatest threat to her life—Soviet Russia

steps forward that it must, in order to yield the maximum crop possible from the available areas, enormous problems must be solved. These are principally industrial problems—the provision of abundant, fairly cheap, home-produced fertilizer; the manufacture in vast quantities of all kinds of farming machinery, from tractors to trucks, from mechanized winnowing machines to pumps. The Chinese have already made very big efforts towards this but—given one of the world's largest, and in some ways most awkward-to-mechanize farmlands, and the absence of any agricultural mechanization before twenty years ago—the task is one of truly enormous proportions.

Equally certain is the course that will be taken by industrialization in China. The continuing shift in balance between heavy and light industry will probably go on, because from one five-year plan to the next the balance probably has to be altered in the light of actual facts. Recent years have shown the Chinese leadership to be extremely adaptable to the changing circumstances both at home and abroad.

Despite industrial expansion and the vast numbers of men and women employed on factory work, despite the propaganda that all and any work, however boring and dull and repetitive, is a worthwhile service to the state, there are some signs in China that in the future this attitude may change. The aim, at a later date, may be to have as few people working in factories as possible. Recent reports from astonished Western industrialists about a car factory in Peking tell of a process there by which cars are manufactured at the rate of about 100 per hour, entirely without the use of human hands. The work is done at all stages by programmed robots with a whole battery of tools fitted to their arms. The robots cannot make mistakes, and can even exercise a limited choice in any given set of circumstances. This is in fact the world's first fully automated car-manufacturing line.

Apart from the technical considerations, there is just the possibility that somewhere, at the back of the planning minds of China today, lies the idea that no one should be forced to work on the shop floor of a factory. It is quite possible that the Chinese think the full life—the full Chinese life—is not possible for people who spend the working part of it in the utter monotony of being human robots in factories. This may sound an extreme suggestion to make at present. But the Chinese are quite capable of such a revolutionary industrial idea. And why bother, in a country where labour is plentiful, trainable and cheap, to design and build this tremendously expensive and intricate first robot factory? It is not as though there was the Western management's nightmare—the strike problem—with which to contend.

But, these matters aside, the largest question-mark must be attached to the future concerning the people and the state. It may be worth quoting at some length the words of an American Chinese, written in 1956 when the new régime was only seven years old. Dr Kuo Ping-chia is far from being a Communist, far from being partisan. What he wrote at that time is without any doubt even more true today. In his book: *China, New Age, New Outlook*, he says:

> The weight of the impact of Communist leadership on the Chinese people lies in the great pertinence of their programme to the existing realities. This is a situation which has repeatedly destroyed conventional ideas and opened up new vistas of unforeseen possibilities.

The author goes on to cite Mao's writings—*High Tide of Socialism in Chinese Villages* (1955), *Ten Great Relations* (1956), together with the Communist Party's *Outline for the Development of Agriculture* (1956)—material that first of all gives the impression

> of being bombastic and unworkable. Yet one by one these plans have now come to be reality. The secret is that the Communists deeply understand the problems of China, and they are capable of applying their programme with a zeal approaching religion. . . . We hear so much about regimentation and state control; but they have led to planning and to the achievement of an orderly purpose. We hear so much about hard labour; but it has yielded a higher productivity; which in turn has ensured growth and security. . . . We hear so much about indoctrination; but it has stimulated discipline, which is sorely needed to promote unity and constructive group endeavour. We hear so much about social levelling; but it has brought in its wake mass education and a wide spread of opportunity, instilling confidence, hope and optimism in the minds of millions of people.

Science has entered into the lives of the Chinese, making a revolution in the attitude to even the smallest and simplest matters of daily existence. The long rule of Confucius, with his doctrines of unquestioning respect for all established authority and for elders, has finally been broken and people have been urged instead to think for themselves within the framework of Marxist-Leninist doctrine. The transition has been stormy, and is far from complete. Twenty-five years ago, few people in China had even heard of the class struggle. Now it is one of the main pivots of thought

The meeting between President Nixon of the United States and Mao was another episode in Chinese diplomatic moves towards an anti-aggression insurance policy. Moscow is and will be for the foreseeable future the potential danger, so Peking takes all steps within reason to protect China from possible Soviet attack. One way is to have most of the world, or at least its informed opinion, on the Chinese side.

An October First parade in Peking. The slogans read from left to right, "Oppose modern revisionism and support Marxism-Leninism." "Oppose United States policy of aggression and war, and defend world peace." "Long live the unity of all peoples in the socialist camp." "Workers of the world unite." These parades have now been suspended —perhaps because they no longer serve a useful purpose. China has no desire or need to show the world her latest armament, no need now to communicate policies by means of such mammoth displays

and action for 800 millions. Without question, the transition from the ingrained outlook of thousands of years to a thoroughly socialist approach to living and thinking could not have been achieved in so short a time, imperfectly achieved as it is, unless a man of the brilliance of Mao Tse-tung had been there to lead the way.

Mao, a man with a soft handshake and a hard head, must surely rank as one of the world's greatest historical figures. At no time in history has so large a number of people at any given time been so deeply influenced in every way by the written and spoken words of one man. The fact that he has had so few dissident voices raised against him within the ranks of the Chinese people, is a reflection not only of that genius which communicates with a kind of mesmeric force, but of his immensely Chinese outlook. Nearly all his published statements have in them, either overtly or by implication, in a turn of phrase, an aspect of thought that any Chinese at once recognizes as Chinese and not just political. One typical example of this is embodied in his frequent statements on all manner of subjects exhorting people to take affairs into their own hands and to use not only new methods but to remember the value of the old ones. The astounding results of this encouragement, which the Chinese never had before, can be seen in every field. The extensive and highly successful work on taming the rivers is the result partly of modern dam technique, but also partly of the massive employment of hydraulic techniques known and used on a smaller scale for two thousand years. Any commune that has straightened the course of a river will proudly remind the visitor not just of the mythical Great Yü, but of the historical personnage Li Ping who, 2,200 years ago, cut through the shoulder of a mountain and not only abolished the ravages of the Min River at Kwansien in Szechuan province but, by a stroke of hydraulic genius, managed to establish a system that irrigated an area of 40 by 50 miles (64 by 80 kilometres) to support a population of about five million people. The system is still fully in use today.

It is not simply a question of instilling some kind of mindless patriotism, but frequently with Mao it is a question of recalling the real achievements of past men and past millions of Chinese people as examples of what can be done. In 1958 Mao said: "Chinese medicine and pharmacology are a great treasure-house, and efforts should be made to explore and raise them to a higher level." We have seen some of the remarkable results of that exhortation.

China and her neighbours

There are other questions that spring to the Western mind when the future is mentioned. One concerns Tibet where some years ago China resumed control of a region for several hundred years under her supervision—a tributary state in which a Chinese government Resident exercised control. It is doubtful if China has any real desire to cope with the thorny problems involved in ruling Tibet. But, the history of the region being what it is—Tibet was really the plaything of Russia and Britain for a century, each power seeking to "neutralize" it on its own side—it would be unreal to expect China, whose claims to rule there are far stronger than those of anyone else, not to take energetic steps to control the destinies of her former tributary state.

And in fact, it must be said that Tibet under China is much better off than under the theocratic despotism of the Dalai Lama and his feudal landlords. When China resumed control of Tibet there was an exhibition in Peking of objects of many kinds just brought from various parts of that Shangri-La on the frozen plateau. I remember a hand or two, embalmed and set on its severed wrist with Tantric symbolism in a Lamaist Buddhist shrine, various objects made of, or covered with, human skin, a horrifyingly real view, in a series of photographs, of how several quite typical Tibetans lived. There is little point in going into the horror of the situation to which most Tibetans were condemned from birth.

The "escape" of the Dalai Lama and his entourage of priesthood, nobility and hangers-on, to India was certainly permitted by China in order to rid the country of at least the focus of major problems. Only Western newspapermen played along with the idea that the spiritual leader of Tibet was escaping the forces of darkness that were closing

The Mao cult as such is on the wane. The redoubtable leader is getting old. The Chinese people, infinitely more politically experienced than they were a decade ago, are a nation so vast, so varied, so numerous, that it is impossible to say at any moment what level of political awareness has actually been reached. Some people may still need a figurehead in the shape of posters of Mao, or the ubiquitous plaster busts of their Great Helmsman

Tibetans in one of the institutes for the national minorities dancing in their national costume. For centuries Tibet has paid tribute to China, and China has had a representative in Lhasa. Tibet has therefore been closely tied to China in a tributary arrangement similar to that linking China and other immediate neighbours. The same sort of links existed with Korea, Vietnam and other countries. Such is the sensitive nature of Tibet's position between India, Russia and China, that it was hardly surprising when China in 1951 took firm control

in from China on his country. In fact it was that priesthood and those aristocratic landowners who had for centuries kept the majority of Tibetans in a state of abject subservience and poverty.

Since then, there has been at least one revolt in a part of Tibet — such is the power of what has become a malign form of religion and of the ingrained feudal system. But there should be no illusions about Tibet. The romantic twaddle written about it simply does not measure up with the facts of the repressive rule of lamas and landlords there. There is nothing romantic or good about an empty belly for most of the time in sub-zero temperatures. One is reminded of the Chinese saying: "an honest magistrate has lean clerks; a powerful god has fat priests". That was Tibet in a nutshell — the priests were fat.

The other question concerns Taiwan. While Chiang Kai-shek's Nationalists are still talking about "liberating China" from Formosa, they have lost their seat at the United Nations to that China, and are gradually being isolated by the withdrawal of recognition by other countries, such as Japan. For China there is no special problem here. Mao always said China would not take her seat at the United Nations until Taiwan had been expelled. It was, and China went to New York. Perhaps the death of Chiang, already in poor health, will eventually solve the problem peacefully, and Taiwan province will be taken back by China.

Hong Kong, an anachronistic colony (once described as a pimple on the backside of China) must seem at first glance to be a glaring example of Chinese double outlook. The staunch anti-colonialists permitting the most colonial of colonies to exist on their own territory. Recent events have made the Chinese view clear. They respect the treaty by which the greater part of Hong Kong is held by Britain, for just so long as it suits them to go on doing so. The convenience of Hong Kong as a modern shipping centre, as an export and import centre run at no expense to China, as a source of millions of dollars in badly needed foreign currency, is such that its use, in spite of Communist views on colonies, is more important than its removal. By the time the lease runs out in 1997, the situation in East Asia, and within China itself, will doubtless be radically altered by various economic and political factors (such as the removal of all American military and commercial power from the area) and Hong Kong may by then no longer hold the attractions of a free port to world commerce.

Of China itself, what has to be considered is the profound effort there to make a new Chinese type of man. The whole process of education, in all its ramifications, in China today is bent towards this end. There is reason for considering the Chinese experiment the most important attempt ever made to alter the manner of thought and action and life of one quarter of mankind in a few decades. The experiment has got off to a very good start, but there is no means of knowing how it will eventually turn out. There is increasing evidence that the nature of mankind is not entirely the product of his physical, emotional and intellectual environment, but that there is a biological factor built in — a legacy of behaviour patterns and other matters from our early human ancestors. No one knows at present how far the kind of alteration in life that China is attempting can actually in the end change the responses of mankind to the circumstances of life. We can all, or maybe nearly all, agree that to make the attempt to alter the national behaviour of a people is a worthwhile experiment in so far as it has, up to now, led to a broad improvement in the standard of life in China.

Recently, quite a large segment of world opinion has begun to drop its hostility and wish the Chinese well. The future for China looks encouraging. No one can now doubt that China will emerge in the not very distant future as a world power of first-class importance — a power with views as direct and intelligent as its long history and its recent Revolution would lead one reasonably to predict.

Men and women of the People's Liberation Army still play an important role in the life of China apart from their military duties. The army helps with commune work, and individuals in the army are continuously at school learning something other than military subjects. The history of the army taking over the state is one that modern China wishes to avoid

ACKNOWLEDGMENTS

Cover photographs by Richard and Sally Greenhill, and Andrew Watson. Endpapers by Mary Evans Picture Library and Richard and Sally Greenhill. Map on page 45 by Leslie Haywood.
Denes Baracs, Interfoto (Camera Press): p. 72. By credit of the Trustees of the British Museum: p. 16 (middle). Camera Press, London: pp. 8, 30, 42–3, 92 (bottom), 96, 99, 106, 121, 125. Nigel Cameron, Rapho Guillemette: pp. 20, 23, 73, 76, 118, 124. China Photo Service (SACU): pp. 38, 95; (Camera Press): 27 (top), 29, 31, 33, 35, 50 (top), 62–3, 66 (bottom), 78, 81, 91 (top), 94 (top), 122. Cooper-Bridgeman Library: p. 16 (bottom). Czech News Agency (Camera Press): pp. 44 (top), 67 (bottom). Mary Evans Picture Library: pp. 9, 11, 18 (top), 19 (top), 54, 91 (bottom), 98. Frank Fishbeck: p. 40. Ciao Garruba (Camera Press): p. 92 (top). Richard and Sally Greenhill: pp. 19 (bottom), 22, 24 (bottom), 25 (bottom), 27 (bottom), 32, 34, 36 (top), 37, 39, 50 (bottom), 51, 55, 65 (bottom), 66 (top), 70 (top), 79, 82, 84, 94 (bottom), 100, 104 (top), 105, 123. Richard Harrington, R.B.O. (Camera Press): p. 104 (bottom). B. O. Heldt (Camera Press): p. 46. Hsinhua News Agency (SACU): p. 47. Shem Lim: pp. 10, 65 (top). Orion Press, Tokyo (Camera Press): p. 64 (top). Picturepoint (K. Hoddle): p. 28 (both). Marc Riboud, Magnum: pp. 15 (top), 60, 69, 80. Society for Anglo-Chinese Understanding: pp. 48, 56, 68, 70 (bottom). Len Sirman Press (Camera Press): p. 58. Doland McCullin, The Sunday Times: p. 26. Times Newspapers Ltd/Robert Harding Associates: pp. 110 (both), 111. Victoria and Albert Museum, London: pp. 7, 17, 18 (bottom), 88 (bottom), 89. Andrew Watson: pp. 25 (top), 49, 57, 59, 75, 85. Roger Whittaker (Camera Press): pp. 52–3.

FURTHER READING

Barnett, A. D. *China After Mao* Princeton and London: Princeton University Press, 1967
Bloodworth, Denis *Chinese Looking Glass* New York: Farrar, Straus & Giroux, 1967. London: Secker & Warburg, 1967; Penguin Books, 1969
Bryan, Derek *The Land and People of China* New York: Macmillan, 1965
Dedmon, Emmett *China Journal* Chicago: Rand McNally, 1973
Gittings, John *A Chinese View of China* London: BBC Publications, 1973. New York: Pantheon Books, 1973
Hunter, Deirdre (Ed.) *We the Chinese: Voices From China* New York: Praeger, 1971
Myrdal, Jan, and Kessle, Gun *China: The Revolution Continued* New York: Pantheon, 1971. Chatto, 1971; Penguin, 1973
────── *Chinese Journey* New York: Pantheon, 1965. London: Chatto, 1966
Schell, Orville, and Esherick, Joseph *Modern China: The Story of a Revolution* New York: Knopf, 1972
Snow, Edgar *Red Star Over China* New York: Grove Press, 1968. London: Gollancz, 1969; Penguin Books, 1972
────── *Red China Today: The Other Side of the River* London: Penguin Books, 1970. New York: Random House, 1971
Spencer, Cornelia *The Land and People of China* Rev. ed. Philadelphia: Lippincott, 1972
Suyin, Han *China in the Year 2001* London: C. A. Watts & Company, 1967; Penguin Books, 1970

INDEX

Figures in italic indicate illustrations

A
Academia Sinica, 111, 113
Achieving Self-Perfection, 79
Acupuncture, 101–7, *101*, *104*, *106*
Agriculture, 21–5, *21*, *23*, *24*, *33*, 37, *37*, 43, *78*, 119
Anaesthesia, 101, 106–7, *106*
Analects of Confucius, 15
Antagonistic contradiction, 51
Archaeology, 101, *103*, *109*, 110–17, *110*, *111*, *117*
Architecture, 61–7, 70, *70*, 87
Arts, *7*, *12*, 14, *14*, 16, *16*, 87–99, 116–17

B
Ballet, *94*, *95*
Banking, 76
Bicycles, 72
Boxer Rebellion, 19, *19*
Bright Star Brigade, 22, 33–4
Brilliant dynasty, 17
Britain, 76, 123–4
Buddhism, 15, *15*, 123
Bund, the, 76

C
Calendar, 7
Calligraphy, 16, 87, *89*, *91*
Cartoons, 95
Central Committee, 30–1
Ch'ang-an (Sian), 11, 14
Ch'ang-an Avenue, 65, *70*, 72
Changsa, 113
Characters, 9, 77
Cheng Ho, 17
Chiang Ch'ing, 89, *96*
Chiang Kai-shek, 19, 124
Chiaoli commune, 22–30, *24*, 33–7
Chin dynasty, *10*
Chin dynasty (non-Chinese), *10*
Ch'in dynasty, *10*, 11
China, New Age, New Outlook (Kuo Ping-chia), 121
Ch'ing dynasty, 7, *10*, 18–19
Chou dynasty, 10, *10*, *12*, *110*, *111*, 113
Chou En-lai, 41, *43*, *44*, 56, *96*
Christianity, 15, *15*, 18
Chu Teh, 41, *43*
Cinema, *46*, 93–5, 99
Clothing, 27–8, *28*
Coexistence, 59
Committees, 30–1, 55–6
Communes, 21–39, *24*, *31*, *32*, 87
Communication, 84, 97, 99
Communist aims, 76
Communist Party, 7, 19, 21, 30, 41, 80, 99
Confucius, 8, *9*, 10, 13, 15, 41
Constitution of China, 42–7
Contradictions, 51–2
"Coolie", 43–4

Co-operatives, 28–30
Cottage industries, 71–2
Cowrie shells, 9–10
Cultural Revolution, 38, 53–8, *53*, *56*, *59*, 73–5, 79–80, 83, 94, 99

D
Dalai Lama, 123
Dams, *76*, *77*, *102*, *107*, 108–10, 122
Diamond Sutra scroll, 16
Diet, 27
Discussion groups, *47*, *48*
Droughts, 37
Duties, 43–4
Dynasties, 8–19, *10*

E
Earnings, 83–5
Education, 26, *27*, 35, 37–9, 58, 74–5, 77, 83
Electoral units, 46
Elgin, Lord, *18*
Emancipation of women, 39

F
Feudal system, 11
Films, *46*, 93–5, 99
Five Dynasties Period, *10*, 16
Five Year Plan, 79
Flag, 42–3, *44*
Floods, 37, 108–10
Food, 84, *85*
Foreign business, 76
"Four olds", 8

G
Gate of Heavenly Peace, 38, 42, *55*, *64*
Genghis Khan, *17*
Goddess of Mercy, *88*
Gordon, General "Chinese", 19
Government, 46, 51, 55–9, 76
Great Hall of the People, 62, *64*, *67*
Great Leap Forward, *61*, 71, 78–80, 83
Great Wall, 11, *12*, 18, 68, *69*
Guo nobility, 111–12

H
Han dynasty, *10*, 11–13, *13*, *14*, 15, 41–2, *111*, 113
Han tombs, 88, *111*
Hangchow, 16, 22, *46*
Hao Jan, 97
Health, *51*
History, 8–19
Holidays, 26–7
Ho Lung, *43*
Hong Kong, *8*, 124
Housing, 51
How to be a Good Communist, 79
Hsi Hsia dynasty, *10*
Hsia Kingdom, *10*
Hydro-electric schemes, 30, *30*, *76*, *77*, *107*, 108–10

I
Ideographs, 8
Imperial Examinations, 13
Imperial Palaces, *62*, *65*
Income, 33–5, 37, 83–4
India, 119
Industrial revolution, 81
Industry, 43, *61*, 70–2, *71*, 76–80, *79*, 83, *83*
Institute for Chinese Medicine, 103, 106
Intellectuals, 98
Inventions, 81–3, *81*, *82*
Irrigation, *35*, 108–10, *108*
Isolation, 119

J
Jade, *103*, *111*, *112*, 113
Japan, 19, 76, *120*
Jin, 23

K
K'aifeng, 16, *81*
K'ang-hsi, 18
Kuan-yin, *88*
Kublai Khan, 17, *17*
K'ung Fu-tzu, *see* Confucius
Kuo Mo-jo, 49
Kuo Ping-chia, Dr, 121
Kuomintang, 41

L
Labour, 80–1
Lamas, 123–4
Landlords, 28, 33, 35, 41, 44, 123–4
Language, 8, 11, 45
Legalists, 11, 13
Liao dynasty, *10*
Liberation of Peking, 70
Lin Piao, 43, 56, *96*
Li Ping, 122–3
Literacy, 35, 77
Literature, 16, 87, 97–9
Little Red Book, *56*, 99
Liu Shao-ch'i, 38, *38*, 42, *43*, 56, 58, 79–80
Liu Sung dynasty, *10*
Loess, 9, *34*, 38
Long March, 55
Lu Hsun, 99

M
Manchu, 18–19
Mandarin, 11, 41
Mandate of Heaven, 19
Mao Tse-tung, 7, 19, 21, 30, 37, *38*, *39*, 41, *41*, *43*, 44, 47, 53–6, *55*, 59, 70, 87, *92*, *96*, 98, 99, 122–4, *123*
Maoist theory, 80
Marco Polo, 17, 22
Marquis of Ta's wife, 113–17, *113*, *115*, *116*, *117*
Marxist-Leninist doctrine, 47, 53, 121
Measures, 23

Medicine, 104–8
Mei Lan-fang, 89, *92*
Minerals, *61*
Ming dynasty, *10*, *16*, 17–18, 41, 119
Ming tombs, 70, *70*, 113
Minorities, 45
Monetary units, 9–10, 33–5
Mongols, 16–18, *17*
Morality, 48–9
Moxibustion, 104
Mu, 23

N
National People's Congress, 42, 44, *44*, 46, 56
Nationalists, 19, 124
Needham, Joseph, 101
Neighbourhood industries, 71–2
Nestorianism, 15, *15*
New elite, 79–80
Nixon, Richard, *121*
Non-antagonistic contradictions, 51–2
Non-Chinese, 45
Northern and Southern dynasties, *10*

O
October First Parade, *55*, *122*
Opera, 87–93, *92*, *93*
Opium, 18
Opium Wars, 18

P
Painting, 87, *87*, *89*, 91, 95–7, *98*, 114
Pandas, 74, *74*
Paper, 13, *83*, 88
Paper Tiger, *98*
Peking, 7, 17–19, 61–74, *62*, *64*, *65*, *66*–7, *70*
Peng Chen, 53
People's Liberation Army, *58*, *125*
People's Republic of China, 19, 44, 46, 64
Pollution, absence of, 72
Population, *45*, 67, 74–5
Porcelain, 13, *13*, 16, *16*, 87, 88
Pottery, 111, 116
Prices, 84
Printing, *16*, *91*
Problems of government, 51
Production, 33, 46, 76, 79, 83
Pure dynasty, 18

R
Railways, 73, 83
Reactionary elements, 51
Red Army, 7, 19
Religions, 15, *15*
Republican China, *10*, 19, *19*
Revolution, The, 7–8, 38–9, 42, 44–7, 81, 119
Revolutionary Committees, 55–6
Rice, 25, *25*, 28–9, 84
Rights, 43–4
Road building, 79
Russia, 65, 76–7, 119, *120*, 123

S
San Men Sha, 109–10
San Tsuen Ling, 111
Science, 29, 101–17, 121
Science and Civilisation in China (Joseph Needham), 110
Scrolls, 16, 87, 96–7
Sculpture, 87, 97
Shang dynasty, 7, 8–10, *10*, *110*, 111
Shanghai, 72, 75–6, *80*, 103
Sheep, 9
Shih Huang-ti, 11
Sian, 11, *15*
Silk Road, 13
Silk worms, 25
Sino-Soviet relations, 65, 76–7, 119, *120*, 121
Sports facilities, 73–4
Sputnik commune, 30–1
Standard of living, 51, *51*, 83–5
Structure of government, 55–9
Students, 53–5, 74–5
Summer Palaces, *68*, 70
Sui dynasty, *10*
Sung dynasty, 10, 13, 16–17, *16*
Sun Yat-sen, Dr, 19, *19*

T
Tai, 45, *73*, *119*
T'ai Ho Tien, 61
T'aip'ing Rebellion, *18*, 19

Taiwan, 124
Talks at the Yenan Forum on Literature and Art, 87, 98
Tanaka, Kakuei, *120*
T'ang dynasty, *10*, 13–17, *14*, *15*
T'ang tombs, 88
Taoism, 11
Technology, 14, 29, *29*, *30*, 81–5, 120–2
Temple of Heaven, 62, *65*
Teng Hsiao-ping, 94
Theatre, 92, 99
Thirteen Tombs, *70*
Thoughts of Mao, *56*
"Three gates", 110–11
Three Kingdoms, *10*
Tibet, 123–4, *124*
T'ien An Men, 62–4
Tombs, 70, *70*, 88, 101, 111 17, *111*
Treaty of Nerchinsk, 18
Treaty of Tientsin, *18*
Ts'ao Hsueh-ch'in, *91*

U
United Nations Organization, 119, 124
United States of America, *121*
Unity of outlook, 47–9

V
Verbiest, Ferdinand, 18

W
Wang Hung-wen, 56
Warlords, 19, 35, 41
West Liao dynasty, *10*
Western attitudes, 48, 87
Western presence, 18–19, 75–6
Writing, 9

Y
Yangtze River, 38, 77, *77*, *102*, 110
Yellow River, 9, 38, *76*, 77, 81, 109–10
Yenan Forum, 87, 98
Yin dynasty, *10*
Yin-yang, 13, 59
Young Pioneers, *41*
Yü (Great), 81–3, 109, 122
Yuan, 33–5
Yüan dynasty, *10*